The biography of John Gibson, R.A., sculptor, Rome

John Gibson, T Matthews

WITHDRAWN

THE BIOGRAPHY OF
GIBSON, R.A., SCULPTOR, ROME

THE TINTED VENUS

THE BIOGRAPHY OF JOHN GIBSON, R.A., SCULPTOR, ROME

BY

T. MATTHEWS

ILLUSTRATED

LONDON: WILLIAM HEINEMANN, MCMXI

PREFACE

THIS biography of John Gibson is largely an
autobiography, being entirely based upon his own
notes and letters and, as far as possible, in his own
words. There can be no doubt that Gibson hoped
that Mrs. Margaret Sandbach of Hafod-un-nos
would write his biography. Mr. and Mrs. Sandbach
visited Rome in 1838 and commenced a life-long
friendship with the famous sculptor. Mrs. Sandbach
had inherited much of the talent of the Roscoes,
and was a writer of considerable ability. As the
grand-daughter of his first patron William Roscoe,
Gibson was predisposed to think highly of her.
Nor was he disappointed. She must have elicited
a promise from him to correspond with her
regularly, to enable her to write a memoir of him.
The letters commence with the year 1839. In
them he writes as to a very intimate friend, indeed,
as to a daughter, laying his heart bare, speaking
quite frankly of his ideas and projects, giving

incidentally an account of current events at Rome.
The idea took more definite shape ten years later.
Gibson explains his intention thus—" I have
thought of writing a few notes upon my early
beginning and progress at Liverpool for you, that
when I am gone to the land of cloudless splendour,
you might write a little memoir of me. What I
write for you would be simply those facts of my
youth, in which you would see a determined
resolution to march on, feelings, affections, enthusiasm, sentiments upon art—you might build
up something useful."

Unfortunately, however, Gibson was not privileged
in that respect, for Mrs. Sandbach died in 1852.
The " notes " which Gibson wrote seem to me to
be such as should, for many reasons, be allowed to
speak for themselves. The man writes without
vanity, without boastfulness, of all that made life
worth living for him—to his most intimate friend.
I have felt that the genius of the man speaks in his
letters and notes. In one, he declares that
" Sculpture is my poetry"; but like many others
of his countrymen, " John of Conway " could also
write beautiful poetic prose. I therefore determined,
in preparing this biography, to give his auto-
biographical notes almost as they were written, and
when those terminate to complete the narrative
from his letters. That was the only way to do him

justice ; John Gibson should explain his "poetry,"
his ideals, for himself—to do aught else would be
to mar a very human document.   May the meed of
blame be mine—John Gibson's the praise.   Later,
I hope to write a critical account of his life and
work.

The photographs from statuary at Marlborough
House are reproduced by gracious permission of
Her Majesty Queen Alexandra.

I acknowledge with gratitude the courtesy of
the President and Council of the Royal Academy
in enabling me to reproduce photographs of the
Gibson statuary at the Royal Academy; to the
Council of the Royal Institution, Liverpool, and
to the Lord Mayor, Aldermen, and Council of
that City for similar privileges , to Mr. Lawrence-
Dibden, Curator of the Walker Art Gallery; to
Dr. Ashby, Director of the British School at
Rome, for being so kind as to permit me to use
certain photographs of his ; to T. J. Barrett, Esq.,
for his generous permission to reproduce the Tinted
Venus ; to Mr. Aneurin Williams, of Carnarvon,
and to Mr. E. W. Evans, Dolgelly, for many
newspaper cuttings and references.

Finally, I wish to express my especial gratitude
to the late Mrs. H. R. Sandbach and to Colonel S.
Sandbach of Hafod-un-nos for allowing me to use
their Gibson papers, to photograph their statuary,

and for many other kindnesses. When the genius of John Gibson shall be adequately honoured, their loyalty to his memory will have a very laige share in that duty; and to Mr. T. H. Thomas, R.C.A., one of the last surviving artist friends of Gibson's at Rome, for much guidance and information.

CONTENTS

CHAPTER VIII

CHAPTER IX

CHAPTER X

CHAPTER XI

CHAPTER XII

CHAPTER XIII

CHAPTER XIV

CHAPTER XV

CHAPTER XVI

CHAPTER XVII

CHAPTER XVIII

CHAPTER XIX

CHAPTER XX

CHAPTER XXI

LIST OF ILLUSTRATIONS

CHAPTER I

INTRODUCTORY —CONWAY.—EARLY ATTEMPTS

THE man who ventures to write about himself
and the intellectual pursuit which has been the
occupation and the ambition of his life, should
reflect whether he has acquired sufficient knowledge and correct taste, and if he has trod in the
true path which leads to excellence.

Sculpture is an art most noble and beautiful,
honoured and encouraged in every enlightened
age. Nature represented in marble is always most
impressive, it enchants and astonishes the multitude. It is the love of my art and the desire of
imparting to the young all the experience which I
have gained in the course of a long period which
induces me to state all concerning my studies
during a residence of forty years at Rome.

My devotion, steady perseverance, and the determination kept up always to make my last work
the best will be recorded ; for my example, in this
respect, may contribute to give courage and hope
to the ambitious youth who may have received
from nature the rare gift of genius.

I will begin from my earliest days to relate every incident which my memory has retained.

Conway, North Wales, is greatly admired for the beauty of its scenery. It was there near the castle I was born in the year 1790, and christened in the parish church.[1] My father and mother were Welsh and we always spoke Welsh—speaking English was a labour to us. My father was a poor man, truly honest. My mother was an excellent woman, passionate and strong-minded; she ruled my father always, and continued to govern us all as long as she lived.

I must first mention the earliest circumstance I can recall to my remembrance, for it was of great importance to me, and ever inspired me with lasting gratitude. One day I entered the house with a cake in my hand, of which I had been eating. My mother's quick eye fell upon the cake and she said, "Who gave you that?" "The woman in the street there, who sells them," I replied. Observing something odd in my manner, she moved slowly to a corner, grasped a rod, and concealed it in the folds of her dress; took me by the wrist, marched me out into the street before the woman. "Did you give this boy a cake?" "No." "Now sir, put you down that cake there."

---

[1] The entry in the Conway Register of Baptisms for that year is — "Baptiz'd John son of William Gibson of the Parish of Gyffin, by Jane Roberts, his Wife, June 19th" Cf Appendix II

I did so, trembling, and immediately the rod fell with the utmost vigour upon my head, shoulders, arms, and hands in presence of the people who were looking on. My distress was very great. At evening prayers my father, who had been informed of my disgrace, dwelt in a solemn manner upon the sin which I had committed—the great crime of theft and lying. That was my first theft, and the last.

I will now relate my artistic beginning. When about seven years old I began to admire the signs painted over ale-houses, and used constantly to gaze up at them with great admiration. One day I made my first attempt to draw a composition from nature; my attention had been frequently attracted to a pretty scene; it was a line of geese sailing upon the smooth glassy water. I drew the geese upon my father's casting-slate all in procession, every one in profile. When my father looked at my performance, he smiled, but when my mother cast her eyes upon the drawing she praised me, and said, " Indeed, Jack, this is very like the geese."

I rubbed out my drawing, and after dwelling upon the reality anew, I drew them upon a larger scale, one behind the other, and again my mother was pleased, and approved and praised me still more. A third time I produced this same subject, adding more geese, but nothing new in the treat-

ment; after receiving still higher praise from my
mother, she said, "Now suppose you change the
subject, and try and draw a horse." After gazing
long and often upon a horse, at last I ventured,
and tried this difficult subject—drew him in profile,
all by memory. This effort surprised and delighted
my mother; she bestowed the highest praise upon
me, and my father expressed his approbation. I
continued to draw the horse, but always in the
same view, when my mother suggested that I
should draw a man upon his back. I then went
out to watch men on horseback, and returning
home, produced an equestrian figure, to the great
delight of my mother. I never thought of copying
from the object itself on the spot, but after looking
long at it, went home, and there drew from
recollection.

CHAPTER II

LIVERPOOL —HIS SCHOOL LIFE AND APPRENTICESHIP —
WILLIAM ROSCOE —THE STUDY OF ANATOMY —THE
D'AGUILAR FAMILY.—JOHN KEMBLE

WHEN I was nine years old my father decided to
join some Welsh people who were emigrating to
America. We arrived at Liverpool to embark for
the United States. When my mother saw the great
ships in the docks, she formed the most determined
resolution never to put her foot in any one of those,
so that my father was obliged to abandon his intention and settle down in Liverpool.[1] I was immediately put to school there, and later, to a higher one.
My attention was shortly attracted to the print-shop
windows, and daily did I return and gaze with
wonder and admiration at the engravings there;
soon I began to draw them The following was
my plan, for I had no money to purchase a print.
I fixed all my attention upon one figure only, and
when it was well impressed upon my mind, I
hastened home, and there sketched down the

[1] They lived, while at Liverpool, in 13 Green Lane, Clarence St —
now demolished

general action—returned again and again to the
original, and then recorrected my copy till it was
finished. I continued this sort of practice for a
long period, and this habit strengthened my
memory wonderfully, which power so important
to an artist, I have had through life. Should I
see any momentary action in the street or
drawing-room, impressing it upon my mind at the
moment and wishing to remember the action, I
can sketch it a month after. In the course of
time I began to sell my drawings to the boys at
school, which enabled me to purchase paper and
colours. I made no profit, for my prices were
small. There was a very amiable boy who was
fond of me, and he always admired my works.
His father had presented him with a new prayer-
book beautifully bound—this gift, with sixpence
from his mother, was for good conduct at school.
The boy said to me, " Gibson, you know how
much I admire your drawings" (he had real love
for the arts) : "if you will make me a drawing in
colours, as a frontispiece for my new prayer-book,
I will give you the sixpence, for my mother gave
me leave to spend it in any way I like." At that
time there was a fine print of " Napoleon Crossing
the Alps," from David, exhibited in one of the
shop windows ; already I had copied this print, I
showed my copy to my patron, he was charmed,
and ordered me to repeat that subject to fit into

his prayer-book , it was done in rich colours, and he paid me the sixpence, the largest sum which I had yet received for a drawing.

I had been warned by the schoolmaster not to draw during school hours; notwithstanding this prohibition, one day at the desk I was discovered drawing by the sentinel when making his rounds. He shouted loud, "Gibson is drawing." The master, full of anger, thundered, "Bring Gibson out." The sentinel said to me, "Obey," and took me by the arm. I resisted—the master then ordered reinforcements—they were soon upon me, when I defended myself and quickly got the worst of it, and received a most severe flogging not to be forgotten, so I never drew again at school.

There was a stationer's shop in Church Street kept by Mr. Tourmeau; it was there I purchased my paper and colours. One day Mr. Tourmeau said, " Young gentleman, you are a good customer, I suppose you are a painter." I replied, with an inward feeling of self-consequence, " Yes, sir, I paint." He then requested me to bring him something to see; I did so, and he said something encouraging, and asked me if I had ever seen an Academy drawing. I did not know what an Academy drawing meant. The following day I saw for the first time in my life drawings from the nude on coloured paper in black and white chalk, done at the Royal Academy by Mr.

Tourmeau; he most kindly lent me his drawings to copy from, and gave me lessons, and when I had advanced myself in the first rudiments, he lent me small plaster casts from the antique and I drew from them under his generous instructions.

The time arrived when I was to be put to a profession. The portrait and miniature painters required a premium with the pupil, which my father could not afford. At the age of fourteen I was bound an apprentice to Messrs. Southwell & Wilson, cabinet-makers. After remaining there one year, I was quite disgusted with my employment, and I succeeded in persuading my masters to change the indenture, and I was bound to them to wood-carving, that is, ornamenting furniture. I was delighted with this occupation, and during my home hours continued to draw from casts. When I had been employed at the wood carving for nearly a year, I became intimate with a person from London; he was a flower carver in marble; his works enchanted me, and soon I became greatly excited. This person presented me to Messrs. Francis, the proprietors of the marble works in Brownlow Hill. They employed a Prussian sculptor to model and to execute small figures which they required, his name was Liege, afterwards he became the head workman to Sir F. Chantrey. No words can give any idea of the powerful impression made upon me by the models and works which I saw there; during the second year of my apprenticeship I modelled in clay, copying what casts I could procure. I soon began to feel the greatest contempt for my profession of wood carving, and became very melancholy. Mr. Francis allowed me to visit his place to see the works, and one day I ventured to ask him if he would allow me to copy in clay a small head of Bacchus by Mr. Liege which enchanted me by its beauty.

When my copy was finished I brought both it and the original to Mr. Francis—he said that it was so perfectly exact that he could scarcely distinguish one from the other—but he gave me to understand that as he had paid a large price to the Prussian sculptor for all the models in his place, he could not allow them to be copied—that he could not lend me any more. Such sentiments, so unexpected and so discouraging, fell upon my ardent soul like the chill of death. I left him in great depression of spirits. I related all to the person who had presented me to Mr. Francis. At that time I had made my first attempt in marble; it was a small head of Mercury, which afterwards I presented to Mrs. Vose.

As Mr. Francis had pronounced my attempts surprising, the idea came into my mind to try and induce Mr. Francis to purchase my indenture from the cabinet-makers, to re-bind myself to Messrs.

Francis, and to serve the remainder of the seven years to them in the practice of sculpture.

My masters would not part with me on any account, alleging that I was the most industrious lad they ever had. At length Mr. Francis was induced to offer them seventy pounds for my indenture, but it was all in vain. I then fell upon a plan to emancipate myself. I attended to the working hours regularly, but did next to nothing of work—I who had been so industrious! They remonstrated with me: " How ungrateful! Have we not treated you always with kindness and so often made you many presents? Can you deny the truth of all this?' I said, " It is quite true." They then tried to persuade me in the kindest manner to return to my former state, and then added, " We could imprison an apprentice for neglecting duty; are you aware of the law?" I replied, " Yes, sir." My resolution was however fixed. A sculptor I must be. " I will fight for it," said I to myself, and I would rather serve the remaining years in prison than continue at wood-carving, an employment which had become disgusting to me

Many days passed on, during which I did scarcely any work, though always at my post. At length my master fell into a rage, called me a most ungrateful scoundrel, gave me a blow on the side of the head, but with his open hand, not violently. I kept myself calm, and said with cool determination, "I am quite prepared to be summoned before the magistrate   I shall have nothing to say in self-defence.   I have made up my mind to stay in prison, yes for years."   In the meantime a third person was employed to persuade them to accept the offer of seventy pounds from Mr. Francis.   At length they were convinced that they never could bring me to work any more for them.   At last the happy day arrived when I was bound an apprentice to sculpture in marble to Messrs. Francis.

I began my delightful employment in high spirits, and I was truly happy, modelling, drawing, and executing works in marble   When I had practised there some months, one day there came a tall magnificent looking old gentleman, his hair was white as snow, aquiline nose, thick brows, benevolent in manner.   Mr. Francis presented me to him. This was William Roscoe.   He came there to order a chimney piece for his library at Allerton Hall. My numerous drawings were soon placed before him and my models : he looked over them all with very great attention, he said many encouraging things to me, and added that he would return soon and see more of me.

In the course of a few days Mr. Roscoe returned and settled with my master about the chimney-piece.   Also he said that I should make a basso-relievo for the centre of it, not in marble, but a model in clay baked (terra cotta); he had brought with him a portfolio out of which he took a print, and showing it to us said, " This is what I wish to be modelled." He said, " This print is of great value; it is by Marc Antonio from Raphael." It represented Alexander ordering Homer's Iliad to be placed in the casket taken from Darius—an excellent choice of subject for a library. The original fresco is in the Vatican painted in chiaroscuro.

I finished my model, which gave the greatest satisfaction to Mr. Roscoe; it has been preserved to this day, and placed in the Liverpool Institution. It is in a small room there, and over it is a portrait of Mr. Roscoe, and also one of myself painted at Rome by the late Mr. Geddes. My portrait was purchased by the late William Earle of Liverpool and presented by him to the Institution Mr. Geddes also painted a repetition of that picture, which was bought by the late Sir Robert Peel and placed by him in his portrait gallery at Drayton.

Mr. Roscoe's kindness became more frequent, and I was invited once a week to Allerton Hall, and there he opened all his portfolios of prints from all the great old masters. He had also a considerable collection of original drawings, for which he had paid great sums. He advised me to copy some of those fine drawings, so that I might learn to sketch in the same masterly manner, and that he would bring one of the most valuable of

ALEXANDER ORDERING HOMER'S ILIAD TO BE PLACED IN A CHEST.

[To face p. 12.

them in a portfolio. Many of those fine things I imitated as near as possible. Some were in red chalk, others in pen, and shaded with bistre. I also copied some of Luca Cambiasi's bold reed pen sketches.

Mr. Roscoe considered it was high time for me to study anatomy from the subject itself, and I felt most anxious to begin, already I had read the life of Michael Angelo and discovered what a great anatomist he was. Dr. Vose was giving lectures on anatomy to many young surgeons at that time; I had the good fortune to be presented to him and he generously admitted me into his school gratis.

My master had accommodated the doctor with a room for his purpose for a few weeks—it was over my modelling room. One night the place had been entered by thieves, and my master determined to have a bed put up there for one of the men to sleep in; to that I objected, saying I should prefer to sleep in the modelling room myself, so it was settled.

How vividly do I remember that dark winter night, when the surgeons brought in a dead body in a sack! I had orders to be there at 9 o'clock to receive them: at half-past nine they arrived with a large sack containing a body; they carried it up into the room, threw it down on the floor, untied it, and emptied its contents; the body lay extended on the ground—it was that of a woman, middle-aged, well-made, but a plebeian face, her long black hair

streaming on the floor, her blue eyes half open, and
her mouth showing her fine white teeth; the expression of the face gave an idea of a painful death.
I had never seen a dead body before, and I felt a
sensation of horror and pity, but I was ambitious to
appear, like the surgeons, indifferent. They threw
the sack over the subject and all retired, I to sup
with my parents who lived near. After supper I
lighted my lantern as usual to go to the studio to
sleep—I had not mentioned the dead woman to my
parents. The night was very dark and I traversed
the large marble yard quite alone, unlocked the
door of the building, entered, and locked myself in
and was soon in the room where I was to sleep, the
lantern I placed on the table, and having a brace of
pistols as a protection against the robbers, I placed
them as usual on the floor close to the bed.

Now had arrived the trying hour which put me
to the proof whether I had really emancipated
myself from a profound and religious belief
imbibed from childhood in Wales—that God did
sometimes permit the spirits of the dead to appear
to the living. How many well-authenticated proofs
of ghosts appearing had I been accustomed to
hear! At this time I was seventeen. "Do I
believe in ghosts?" said I to myself. "No—no."

As I slowly undressed to go to bed, I cast up my
eyes at the ceiling of my bedroom. Yes, just over
my head, stretched on the floor, was the body of

the dead woman. When I had undressed, it struck me that my lantern had better be left to burn—it would be more pleasant, but this indulgence was contrary to my habits. I looked at the bright, dear little blaze which cast its cheerful light around me in that most isolated place with feelings which I could not account for—fear—no—no, no fear, said I, and blowing out the light, I jumped into bed, soon closed my eyes, expecting to fall asleep as usual in a quarter of an hour Two hours passed on, and no sleep. I often changed my posture—first on the right side, then on the left. The closer I kept my eyes, the more distinctly did I see the dead woman with her half-opened eyes, her relaxed jaws, her white teeth, and her long, dishevelled hair; there she lay, stretched before me. Whichever way I turned, there she appeared. Another hour and another is announced by the watchman, still no sleep—" Is this fear?" said I—" no—no, I fear not." "There—there she is again; there is no flying from her. To-morrow she will be under the hands of the surgeons." Such thoughts as these kept me awake, till at length exhausted nature was softly sinking to rest, when, all of a sudden, I was roused up by a noise like a crash over my head where the dead woman lay. "What can that be?" I was puzzled to death, a cold chill came over me; I put my hand to my forehead and felt the cold perspiration. " Do 1 then fear? No—yes, dare I not look at a ghost ?—Appear now before me." "There must be robbers in the place" said I, and leaped out of the bed, seized hold of my pistols expecting every moment to find the door of my room burst open. I stood ready to fire—no noise, everything was silent as the grave—awful silence ! even the buzzing of a fly would have cheered me. Everything was asleep but myself. At last I put down my pistols and went to bed and soon fell fast asleep. When I awoke in the morning the first thing I did was to go to the room above to ascertain the cause of the noise which had so agitated me. The first thing I found there was a fine large cat, who it would appear had thrown down a marble basso-relievo which had been placed on its broad edge on the shelf of one of the chimney pieces, and it was a little distant from the wall, so that puss had got between it and the wall. During the day I drew the face of the dead subject as large as life, and I have the drawing still by me, and it is drawn with freedom and truth , it bears the date 1813. The surgeons soon began to dissect the body, and I made drawings. This important study I practised for three years under Dr. Vose.

After the doctor had finished his lectures for the season, without his knowledge I joined several students to rob dead bodies from their graves, for at that time there was great difficulty in obtaining subjects for the study of surgeons, the law being then so severe against robbing graves that if we had been discovered the magistrates would have been obliged to carry the law into effect, and the poor people would have exercised their vengeance upon us ; but, notwithstanding all the dangers, our enthusiasm for that study made us bold, and fortune was propitious.

There was one of the public burying places a little out of town, still, the houses were so near that we could hear the voices of the women and children. The coffins were laid in a deep trench in lines one upon the other, the whole being covered over with boards. One of us was appointed to go and watch during the day for a funeral and to give us notice. On this occasion, before nine o'clock, we reached the place with a horse and sack. We had a dark lantern. When we got over the wall into the burying-ground we removed one or two boards which covered the deep trench, then went down the ladder, and we were surrounded by the dead in their coffins, which were placed in lines one on the other ; the last on the row was the one newly brought there ; that we opened, and there lay the body of a very beautiful girl about sixteen : her face was full and round How sweet and innocent she looked in death ! She was shrouded in white linen, and sprinkled over with bits of red wool like flowers. We passed our dark lantern round about

c

her face and all felt admiration and sympathy. We
then reclosed her coffin, not wishing to disturb the
body. The next coffin we opened was that of a
fine young man. So we soon had him in our sack,
and lifting him out of the trench, we immediately
got over the wall The sack was then placed on
the horse, and the strongest of our party rode
behind it, he was dressed like a common fellow,
and so were the others, in disguise. The following
winter I joined again in that dangerous and horrid
work, and great was my delight when this practice
was over.

I had completed my anatomical education and
was well versed in the structure of the human body ;
any anatomical error in a work of art I could detect
at a glance. Doctor Vose continued my kind
friend as long as he lived, he had great love for art,
and Mrs. Vose drew the figure, etched on copper
and modelled. She is living, and her only son,
Dr. Vose, is considered a clever young man, and
has considerable practice at Liverpool.

Mr. Francis, my master, was no artist, nor had
he any one who could teach me my profession ; he
was a man of business only and had employed
Mr. Liege to sculpture for him, and as I advanced
rapidly he no longer required his services. I was
paid six shillings per week ; but my master received
good prices for my works.

Mr. Roscoe was a man of true taste and judg-

ment in art ; I have been convinced of that through
life when I remember all his remarks. Every design
which I made was laid before him for his advice.
The first thing which he considered was whether
the subject was expressed simply, clearly, and
naturally ; if the figures moved and acted as nature
would, with truth of character and just expression,
also, he well discriminated whether the subjects were
well selected for representation. Having free
access to his extensive collection of old prints from
the greatest masters, I became well acquainted with
the designs and inventions of Raphael and Michael
Angelo. The genius of the latter began to exercise
considerable influence over me. I made some
designs from Dante's " Inferno." The principal
cartoon which I spent much time upon is a figure
nearly life size. The sinner is worried by a serpent,
the action is difficult, but every part of the figure
is from nature and also shaded like a picture in
black chalk. This cartoon is preserved, and is in
the possession of Mr. Mayor, goldsmith, at Liverpool, he is a man of taste in painting and sculpture.
After an absence of twenty-seven years from
England I saw this cartoon, and I must confess
that that work surprised me to find that I had
advanced so far at that period. Mr. Mayor has
also collected several drawings of a small size for
me during that time.

Before I was nineteen I began a large cartoon,

the subject was the fall of Satan with his Angels.
There are groups and single figures falling in every
way I could think of, and the drawing is all in light
and shade, done with pen and bistre. There are
figures foreshortened in various ways, and the mode
I adopted was, I modelled the principal groups,
and some of the single figures, and then hung them
up with a string, taking my view, drew from the
model and put in the shadows, then traced my
drawing upon the cartoon till the whole was got in.
The upper figures receive the light from above, and
the lower groups from Hell as the flames begin to
rise. The little models of the figures near the
flames were shaded by placing a lamp below, so
that I obtained a correct and beautiful effect.
Previous to beginning the large work I had drawn
the design small, that having gone through
numerous changes. I of course used nature as
much as possible, and this most laborious early
performance has been preserved in the Liverpool
Institution. It has been sent this year (1856) to
Mr. Hogarth, Haymarket, London, to be cleaned
and repaired.

Mr. Roscoe had already given me serious advice
as to the course which I was to take in order
to become a sculptor. He would frequently say,
"No one can be a greater admirer of Michael
Angelo than I am myself, but I must remind you
that you are a sculptor; and to arrive at excellence

THE FALLEN ANGELS.

(From the Cartoon at the Royal Institution, Liverpool.)

in that art there is only one road—it is that which
leads to the principles of the Greeks; they carried
that department of art to the highest perfection.
Michael Angelo, with all his powerful genius,
missed the purity of the Greeks. It is therefore
their principles which you are to imbibe; the
principles they established from nature must be the
object of your study, but it is the works of the
Greeks that will teach you how to select the
scattered beauties which nature displays. The
Greek statue represents nature in the abstract,
therefore when we are contemplating their sublime
works we feel elevated."

I began to study all casts, gems and prints from
the Antique which I could procure. I modelled a
Psyche which was much liked; she was represented
admiring a butterfly, and it was as much in the
Greek style as I could make it. I could not
pursue my profession—the study of the beautiful—
without the participation of women. My Mother
was the first who praised and animated me
"Now, Jack, we have had enough of the Geese, try
a horse." "Now draw a man upon his back."
Thus little by little she spurred me on.

The family of Solomon d'Aguilar, of Liverpool,
was one of the most accomplished there. Mrs
l'Aguilar was the handsomest old lady I ever saw
in my life; she had been a celebrated beauty.
The late General d'Aguilar was their son, and Mrs.

Lawrence was their highly gifted daughter. Her poetry, both translated and original, is published. She was very handsome, amiable, and possessed the most delightful manners. Mrs. Lawrence was the intimate friend of Mr. Roscoe, and through him I became acquainted with that accomplished family. Mrs. Lawrence had a natural taste for the arts, and often came to see my works, and purchased from time to time some of my small figures in "Terra Cotta," which she has preserved to this day. Through life she has felt the warmest interest in my welfare, and has mentioned me in her published works. She has written many a kind letter to me. In one of mine to her I said, "You have lived to see your Brother, your Son and your Sculptor Generals—am I not a General among sculptors?"

I must have been nineteen when the first exhibition of modern pictures was got up at Liverpool: the first artists of London sent their works there. I had there my model life-size of Psyche and some drawings. The committee invited a writer of articles on art to come from London and review the Exhibition and to draw public attention to it. I forget his name; he brought letters to Mr. Roscoe who directed his attention to my numerous compositions. When it was the turn of my works to be noticed by him, he brought me forth very conspicuously. I remember he said, "This youth has begun where so many have left off." I now regret that I did not preserve those articles.

The first exhibition at Liverpool being open, one day there I observed a group of ladies drawing towards the place where I stood It was Mrs. Lawrence. A lady stood next to her who attracted my attention, particularly when Mrs. Lawrence said, "My sister, Mrs. Robinson." I bowed and fixed my eyes upon her, and was so struck with the beauty and magnificent appearance of the lady. She spoke to me in a low tone, but so gentle, and in the sweetest voice I ever heard in my life; her black eyes were remarkable for their softness. I will give a more particular description of Mrs Robinson further on. She was older than myself by some years.

For days the splendid lady was present and before my mental sight On the Friday following I received an invitation from Mrs. Robinson to take tea at her parents' house on Sunday evening. When the time arrived, and on my way there, my spirits brightened up and flagged by turns. I feared she would find me stupid, and be disappointed. When I arrived I felt agitated. I was conducted towards the drawing-room, and no sooner was my name announced than Mrs. Robinson stepped forth out of the drawing-room and met me in the passage, giving me both her hands, which I pressed with warmth. Her bracelets and chains of gold jingled

with the rustling of her silks as she led me on
gracefully into the room, and she filled the air with
a delicious perfume. After I made my bow to the
lady of the house, Mrs. d'Aguilar, and to some
others, Mrs. Robinson said, "Come, sit by me."
We sat apart from the company, and she kept me
for a long time in conversation, making me feel quite
at my ease, and I discovered as we proceeded in
conversation, that she had a natural taste for the
beautiful in art and also in poetry, and English
classical literature. She was in fact a lady of an
elegant and accomplished mind. I saw that she
was beautiful and I could not doubt that she had a
sweet temper. It was impossible that I could sit
before her without admiration, and I felt that she
was like a gift from the gods

Mrs. Robinson was rather tall, of a dark complexion, jet black hair, fine black eyes with remarkably long eyelashes, the nose was Grecian, and so
was the mouth, with a short, pouting upper lip, and
what a smile ! The gently formed chin finished the
oval of her high-bred countenance, and her noble
figure was full of grace.

As time advanced and I became more at ease
with my kind friend, one evening I ventured to
describe the impression which the first sight of her
made upon me in the exhibition rooms. She said,
" I did observe your emotion very soon, for when

you spoke to me you changed colour." I said that
I felt as if I were in the presence of a goddess.
She then observed, " Persons of your pursuits and
poets are peculiar beings, and must be allowed
greater latitude ; they are always imaginative." I
will return again to the kind and generous partici-
pator of my labours and fame.

John Kemble frequently came to Liverpool, and
the d'Aguilars were his great friends. They requested him to come to see my works : he came and
I felt much encouraged by all he said. He greatly
admired a little figure of a sitting Mercury which
my brother Solomon was then modelling, and I do
now say that it is a remarkable work for a boy of
sixteen. The figure is sitting, but you feel that
Mercury will be up in a moment and fly into the
skies

When Lord Colbourne was in Holland, he one
day turned into a curiosity shop, and he saw this
little Mercury in bronze, but the shopman could
not tell him who the artist was or where it was
cast in metal. His Lordship admired the figure so
much that he purchased it at once. When it was
seen at his house in London some artist told him
that it was by my brother at Liverpool. When I
dined with Lord Colbourne in 1851 he showed me
the Mercury, and asked me if it was an original by
my brother, and I told him all about it, and how

John Kemble admired it when it was still in the clay.

John Kemble was requested by the d'Aguilars to sit to me for a small bust; he kindly consented, and I soon began the work at his lodging. All the time he sat he had a looking-glass in his hand, and, frequently examining his face, corrected me. As I advanced the model—and it was finished greatly to his satisfaction—the d'Aguilars and all his friends gave me great praise. Mr. Kemble sent a cast of the bust to Mrs. Siddons and one to Sir Thomas Lawrence, also one to his brother. I sold many casts to his numerous admirers. Mine is the only bust modelled of that great actor.

I have often thought that if my Cartoon from Danté and the one of the falling Angels, with so many figures and groups in great variety of foreshortening with my models in plaster, could be seen together by judges, I feel convinced that they would give me credit for having done so much in a town where neither Art was cultivated nor any Academy existing; but at the same time I must confess that the collection of Mr. Roscoe and his counsels, versed as he was in the Philosophy of the Art, were to me an academy.

If my cartoons were more pictorial than sculptural, those efforts exercised my imagination to a great degree. Invention was my constant

delight, and has been through life; I have drawn
more than sculptors do generally. When Mr.
Roscoe advised me seriously to form my style
upon the Greeks' simple actions and pure forms,
my taste became less rich, less various—in fact, less
original. I will take up the term *original* again
farther on.

CHAPTER III

As time advanced Mr. Roscoe suggested among
his friends that some plan should be devised to
enable me to go to Rome to study, for he looked
upon Rome as the great University of Sculpture
on account of its splendid collections and the
great assemblage of artists from all parts of
Europe. He considered that I had already given
remarkable promise, that my perseverance was
very great, and, if my life should be spared, he
believed that I should distinguish myself. Such
suggestions from him inflamed my soul with
ambition. Rome was ever in my thoughts, and I
became harassed by anxiety, and often passed
sleepless nights. "Mother," said I, " last night I
dreamt a dream " (she could interpret dreams).
" Well, mother, I dreamt that I was wandering in
solitary meditation when a colossal eagle darted
down upon me, and took me up in the air. Higher
and higher he flew with me, over towns and rivers,

28

till at last I lost sight of the earth, and saw nothing but clouds; fear was upon me, when the earth began to reappear and I felt myself descending. I saw below me a very large town. The eagle alighted with me in the middle of this great town and flew away, people crowded around me with wonder. I cried out aloud, 'Where am I? where am I?' and the people shouted, 'This is Rome!' 'Oh, Rome! Rome! Rome!' cried I aloud." "Jack," said my mother, after deep thinking, "as sure as thou art sitting here before me now, thy fate will carry thee over every difficulty to Rome." As I no longer believed in ghosts, I had lost faith in the interpretation of dreams, but I did not dare to doubt my mother's prophetic powers; indeed, I allowed myself to feel that her prophecy was like refreshing dew falling upon my anxious and often languishing hopes.

The three unmarried daughters of Surgeon Park, of Liverpool, were ladies highly cultivated, and Miss Ann drew and painted with great talent; they became my attached friends, and were most anxious for my advancement and fame; they, and Mrs. Vose, the wife of the Professor of Anatomy, as well as Mrs. Lawrence and her sister, Mrs. Robinson, kept in view the eagle that was to carry me over to Rome; but I had still considerable time before me to fulfil my engagement to my master.

One day the late Sir John Gladstone, father of William Gladstone, M.P., who at that time resided at Liverpool, came and ordered a costly chimney-piece from my master, on the sides of which I executed in alto-relievo two female figures, and Sir John Gladstone made me a present of ten guineas; he preserved that work ever after, and before his death he had the chimney-piece brought to Scotland.

Mrs. Robinson did not reside at Liverpool, but came there to visit her parents, and as time advanced her friendship always increased for me; every new design which I made was laid before her. She was of opinion that subjects from Danté representing the terrible was an effort not natural to me. "I know your nature—subjects of beauty and tenderness would be executed more readily and more gracefully by your chisel. I do not mean that you should not treat the heroic, for such subjects tend to elevate the understanding, and in fact they belong to the highest department of Art." She had a plan in view to read to me—poetry and prose—for the purpose of enriching my mind and employing herself.

The day arrived when Mrs. Robinson was to leave us for a while. When she was gone, I felt her loss deeply, for she had spread around my existence a new charm. In parting she said, " Be happy. Soon you shall have a letter from me." And so our correspondence began, and continued to the end of her days. In the course of time my handwriting became so like hers that one day Mrs. Lawrence said that it was so like Emily's hand that she could not tell one from the other.

I continued to practise my art upon those principles which Mr. Roscoe impressed upon my mind; all was Greek simplicity and pure form. The works of Flaxman in outlines began to delight me, I admired the beauty and purity of his female figures and the heroic nobleness of his Heroes. Although he formed his style upon the Greek Vases, his designs are full of original conceptions.

I made a drawing of Psyche carried by two Zephyrs, afterwards I modelled my design in basso-relievo, and finished it very highly, and had the courage to send it to the Royal Academy Exhibition. This was my first work sent there. Mr. Flaxman had never seen me, but he was so much pleased with my basso-relievo, that he obtained a conspicuous place for it, near the window—in a very beautiful light. I shall have more to say upon this subject when I get on my journey.

Mr. Roscoe was pleased to see me continuing to advance in the pure classical style, and I began to feel more and more the charm of that refinement which began to dawn upon me; but to penetrate further into the principles and practice by which art is perfected I must go into the great world of art and come in contact with rivals—it is by comparing ourselves with others, that we advance and gain victories. At Liverpool I felt like one chained down by the leg, panting for liberation, ever longing to join in the race for the green branch, the laurel crown. The plan to send me to Rome for three years was not so easily accomplished. The rich at Liverpool did not then concern themselves much about art. But although Mr. Roscoe's Bank had failed, and my friends were not rich, still my hopes continued bright, for I had a presentiment that the Eagle would receive commands from Fate to carry me to Rome.

The time arrived when I felt greatly elated, for Mrs. Robinson was soon to return among us. It was in the morning I received a note from her, announcing her arrival, and fixing the hour of meeting. On this occasion she did not reside at her parents' house, but lodged near to them. The moment I was in her presence I felt as if I were fixed to the ground, and she stood still as a statue, beautiful and noble. In silence she advanced, putting forth both hands; so did I. She was dressed in black velvet with her rich gold Indian ornaments, brought from India, where she had lived after her marriage. Her manner was very uncommon, she lived retired and liked solitude; she was of a gentle and sweet disposition. Her indolent, languid movements gave a peculiar grace to all her actions.

There was a mournful tenderness in the silvery tones of her voice when her sympathy was touched, and not unfrequently a shade of sadness in her down-cast looks, which were again brightened by the animation which flashed from her fine eyes fringed round by her long black eye-lashes, and the inexpressible sweetness of her smile. She never was uncharitable in her sentiments towards others and she had a most generous nature.

I had presented some original designs to Mrs. Robinson, and one was greatly admired by her, it represented Hero mourning over the dead body of Leander. I drew this over again at Rome, and it is engraved among my designs published by Hogarth. Soon after her return I made a drawing of the meeting of Hero and Leander, and presented it to her, and she had it framed and kept it in her room. I made a copy of the drawing, and at Rome I showed it to Canova, and he was greatly pleased with the conception of the subject, and advised me to model it. I asked him if it was an objection that the face of the woman was hid in the neck of her lover, not seen, and he said—no, that it was most natural. "It is full of passion," said he. "You must make a basso-relievo of it." I followed Canova's advice, and taking the greatest pains, finished my model; and when the Duke of Devonshire came to Rome and saw my meeting of Hero and Leander, his Grace ordered me to execute it in marble for him, and he has placed it in his Gallery of Sculpture at Chatsworth.

Mrs. Robinson read to me in the evenings as often as circumstances permitted, selecting beautiful passages in prose and poetry, whatever was ennobling in sentiment or enriched the mind with ideas.

Having finished my apprenticeship with Mr. Francis, I soon began to think of leaving Liverpool. Once London was my ambition, but my soul was now all on fire for a higher flight. Golden Hope inspired me, and pointed to the Capitol.

In the year 1817 I left Liverpool for London; I had a letter to Mr. Brougham (afterwards Lord Brougham) and one to Mr. Christie the auctioneer, a man of classical learning. and great taste in art I had taken with me a thick roll of my original drawings, and Mr. Christie examined them very minutely, he said that he would introduce me to Mr. Watson Taylor. The day was fixed for me to go with him, and Mr. Christie desired me to bring all my designs.

Mr. Watson Taylor received me very kindly and he looked over my compositions very attentively, Mr. Christie remaining in the room all the time. It was agreed that I should model a bust of Mr. Taylor, and Mr. Christie was greatly pleased at the success of his introduction. I began the model, which I completed to the great satisfaction of Mrs Watson Taylor and of her friends. They said that it was a more pleasing bust than the one lately done by Mr. Chantrey, so Mr. Taylor desired me to execute the bust in marble. This was the first commission I had after leaving Liverpool.

My success induced Mr. Taylor to have a bust of his wife by me. She sat, and of course I did my utmost, and the model gave the greatest satisfaction, and it was ordered to be done in marble. Then I modelled the children, also to be done in marble.

I made known that it was my intention to venture on my journey to Rome, but I was aware that these busts would prolong my stay in London at least six months or more, which would bring me to the end of September, the best time, I had been informed, to go to Rome after the heat. All this I had made known to Mrs. Robinson, and she very soon came up to London and took a residence there. She had procured a letter of introduction to Canova for me from her brother the late General d'Aguilar. I had also a letter from Mr. Roscoe to Mr Fuseli, in London, who received me very graciously and encouraged me to repeat my visit to him, which I accordingly did. He gave me a note to Mr. Flaxman, who was very kind to me in his turn and most polite. He praised my drawings, agreeing, in that respect, with Mr Fuseli, and complimented me upon my basso-relievo of Psyche and Zephyrs.

The following letter I then addressed to Mr. Roscoe :—

" Since my arrival in London I have often been on the point of writing to you, but my consciousness of the nature of your late engagement rendered me diffident of addressing you.

" Now, as I imagine the bustle of things has subsided with you, I venture to tell you that Mr. Fuseli received me as you could wish, and will give me a letter to Canova, and to others at Rome, and that I have been introduced by Mr. Christie to Mr. W. Taylor, who has employed me since my arrival in London. He is kind, liberal, and rich, and is, I think, determined to be of use to art in all its departments. He has expressed himself particularly delighted with what I have done for him—three busts of his children in marble. At present I am with him and his family at Earl Spencer's villa, modelling his lady and himself. When these are finished I go on to Rome.

" It is with the consciousness of the pleasure this will give you that I thus write about myself This consciousness is more fixed and heightened within me when I count the years you have honoured me with your attention and kindness.

" Whenever my imagination glides to Allerton, it is with deep feeling of gratitude and respect, for it was there my inexperienced youth was led to the path of *simple art* ; it was there it caught the flame of ambition, it was there the suggestion of Rome was given birth to Therefore, dear Sir, though fate has prevented you from indulging your

generous intentions towards me on this occasion of
going abroad, it has not lessened my gratitude, but
has made me feel and value with more warmth the
superior part of our nature, that divine generosity
which, when deprived of those partial gifts of
fortune, exists the same in the noble mind, and
therefore ought to possess a superior, an exalted
place in the estimation of true gratitude. Through
life, dear Sir, gratefully and respectfully yours,

"JOHN GIBSON."

Mr. Roscoe wrote in reply—"I received no
small degree of pleasure and gratification from
your obliging letter, as well from your kind
remembrance of me as from the favourable account
you gave me of your own proceedings and prospects.
As to what you are so good as to say respecting
the advantages you suppose you have derived from
my acquaintance I cannot but be sensible with
what caution I ought to receive it; but I will not
deny that it affords me sincere pleasure, from the
consciousness that it has ever been my wish to
contribute, as far as in my power, to bring forward
those talents, which if patiently and duly cultivated,
will confer lasting honour on your name.

"I rejoice to find you have now met with a friend
who knows how to appreciate your merits. This
morning I had the honour of a letter from Mr. W.
Taylor, requesting that you would take a model of
me for a bust in marble to be executed by you at
Rome—a request which, under such circumstances,
it is impossible for me to refuse As I cannot,
however, leave home at present, I should be glad

of a line informing me when and where you can enter upon this undertaking : and remain with the sincerest esteem and best wishes, etc., etc.

" W. R."

I returned to Liverpool and modelled the bust of Mr. Roscoe. It was done in marble at Rome for Mr. W. Taylor, and a repetition of it for myself, which I presented to the Liverpool Royal Institution, accompanying it with the following letter.

" ROME, *5th March*, 1827.

" SIR,

"Permit me to offer through you to the Committee of the Royal Liverpool Institution (as a grateful tribute to my first patrons, and those who enabled me to study my profession, where I could best learn it) the accompanying bust, in marble, of their illustrious and venerable President, Roscoe.

"To that gentleman I am indebted for what little merit I may possess as a sculptor. He first inspired me with ideas worthy of my profession, and kindled within me an ardent love of fame in the pursuit of it.

"By this monument, if I have endeavoured to perpetuate the lineaments of an excellent man, I hoped also to perpetuate the gratitude and respect of the artist whom he protected.

I have the honour to remain, Sir,
Your much obliged humble servant,
JOHN GIBSON."

T. MARTIN, Esq.,
Secretary, Liverpool Royal Institution.

I had also a letter from Mr. Roscoe and Mr. Fuseli in London, who received me graciously, and he encouraged me to repeat my visits to him, which I did. He gave me a note to Mr. Flaxman, who in his turn was very kind to me and most polite. He praised my drawings as did Mr. Fuseli, also Mr. Flaxman complimented me upon my basso-relievo of Psyche and Zephyrs.

Mr. Flaxman encouraged me strongly to go to Rome, saying, that there I should be in the best school in Europe, surrounded by the finest works, and by artists of all nations, and there I should have the opportunity of becoming known to the rich English patrons who crowded to Rome every winter, and that Canova was generous to young artists of talent.

I waited upon Mr. West, president of the Royal Academy, and after looking over my drawings, he said, "There is that in them which labour can never attain." I cannot but regret that my memory does not retain more of what fell from this celebrated man on that occasion.

I also presented myself without a note of intro-duction to Mr. Blake, after showing him my designs, he gave me much credit for the invention which they displayed; he showed me his cartoons, and complained sadly of the want of feeling in England for high art, and his wife joined in with him and she was very bitter upon the subject.

I did not see Mr. Chantrey, but went round his studio. Mr. W. Taylor said that he had been to Mr. Chantrey in order to talk to him about my going to Rome, for the sake of study, but Mr. Chantrey did not think that there was any necessity for a sculptor to go there, he thought that in London might be found every requisite for his improvement—that I might go to Rome later in life.

I was surprised to hear such an opinion, and I said that I should be guided by the advice of Mr. Flaxman which he had already given to me, who having studied at Rome for seven years, therefore had experience of the advantages there, and that artists from all parts had flocked to Rome for the last three hundred years.

I had finished the busts of the children in marble and Mr. W. Taylor said that he would do all he could to advance me. This was generous, and I expressed my gratitude to him. My means to go to Rome were limited, and the offer of Mr. W. Taylor was a great inducement to me. I thought by prolonging my stay I might meet with encouragement and increase the sum of one hundred and fifty pounds which my friends at Liverpool had got together for me; but when I remembered my dream of the eagle and my mother's prediction I decided not to loiter too long on the way but trust to fortune and depart.

One day I said to my kind friend that the time was drawing near for my departure; he said " Will you not stay to execute Mrs. W. Taylor's bust in marble and my own?" I requested his permission to send on the models to Rome and to execute them in marble there. He still thought that I might stay, but I said that I would go on to Rome if I went there on foot. He remarked that I was very decided indeed.

Mrs. Robinson's plan was that I should stay in Rome two or three years; then return and have my studio in London, and that she would fix her permanent residence near to me for the remainder of her life.

I had formed a friendship with Joseph Bonomi,[1] and Mrs. Robinson allowed me to present him to her, and he made me acquainted with Mr. Nollekens who was then very old, and he highly approved of my going to Rome.

[1] The younger—the Egyptologist and architect He assisted Owen Jones in the decoration of the Egyptian Court of the Crystal Palace.

CHAPTER IV

ROME — HIS RECEPTION BY CANOVA — CANOVA'S STUDIO.
— THE ACADEMY OF ST LUKE'S — THE SLEEPING
SHEPHERD BOY

I LEFT England for Rome in September 1817.
My friend Mr. Bonomi has procured for me a letter
to Mr. Bartolozzi who was then residing at Paris
with his daughter Mme Vestris. She was ill in bed,
and I did not see her. but he was remarkably kind to
me, taking me about the town. I could not speak
any language but English and Welsh, the latter,
however, was of no use to me in Paris.

In the course of a few days, Mr. Bartolozzi found
a Roman Vetturino, who was on his return to
Rome. This circumstance was most fortunate for
me, and my place was taken for Rome in company
with a young Scotchman, who had a servant, and
he could speak French, English and Italian, so I
was taken care of. There was also another Vettura
going in company with us as far as Milan, and in
that was Madame Pasta with her young husband
and her mother. Mr. Graham, the young

Scotchman who was so kind to me all the way, remained at Florence, and I proceeded on to Rome. In the Vettura there was an Italian who spoke a little English, and he was very kind to me all the way to Rome.

On the 20th October, 1817, I arrived at Rome, and my mother's interpretation of my dream was fulfilled.

I had a letter to the Abbé Hamilton, and I found him a good-natured old man. The following day he accompanied me to Canova. When the hour came, I felt anxious and agitated at the idea of seeing the first sculptor in the world.

We arrived at Canova's studio, and as we walked through the rooms crowded with his works, I thought that I had wonderful performances to contemplate. We arrived at Canova's own room, and the Abbé presented me to him, and I delivered the three letters—one was written by Mr. Fuseli, R.A., another by Lord Brougham, and the third by the late General d'Aguilar, the brother of Mrs. Robinson. Canova examined my compositions, looking very much at each, and gave me great encouragement by the manner in which he expressed himself; he said to me in the presence of the Abbé: "I wish you to come to me alone next Sunday morning, for I want to talk with you."

When Sunday morning arrived, I waited upon

Canova at his studio ; there I found a crowd of young artists; some were showing their designs, others talking to him. When he observed me he advanced, and said : " As soon as I have dispatched these persons I will speak to you." When they were gone, he took me to a small room and began in his very bad English to give me to understand that many young artists came to Rome to study with very little means. " That," said he, "may be your case ; as I have assisted many young men I trust that you will allow me to have the gratification of contributing any sums out of my purse to enable you to study to the best advantage and that requires means. I am rich," said he, " and money is of no object I am anxious to be of use to you, and forward you in your art as long as you are in Rome."

It appears that General d'Aguilar in his letter had requested Canova to put me upon the most economical plan of study, saying that my means were very small. I had no doubt, therefore, that his attention had been fixed upon that part of the letter. I was taken by surprise, and I felt it difficult to find words to express my grateful feelings. I told him when I arrived in London that I was introduced to a patron Mr. W. Taylor, and that he had increased my means a little. " Well," said he, " if I see that you study your art with zeal and improve. I will bring you to the

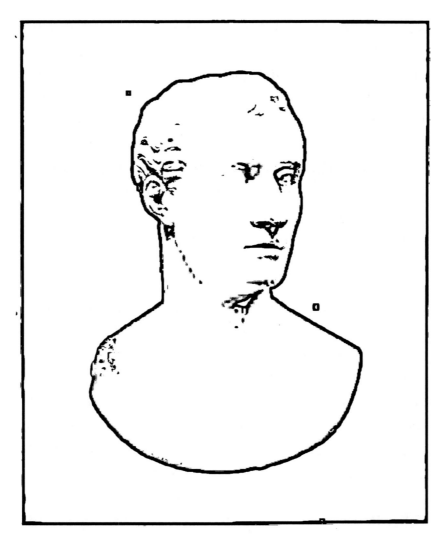

CANOVA

(by himself)

notice of the rich English who come here." I
replied that as he was so generous, I should be
happy to look up to him for instruction ?—to be his
pupil, and to model in his studio ? He said " Yes,"
you may look to me for everything you desire."
Canova's manners delighted me, his gentleness and
his deep sonorous but soft voice; his very fine-
formed features. prominent forehead and deep-sunk
expressive grey eyes.

Dear generous master, I see you now before me.
I hear your soft Venetian dialect, and your words
of encouraging praise inspiring my efforts and gently
correcting my defects—yes—my heart still swells
with grateful recollection of you.

In a few days John Gibson of Conway was
modelling in the studio of the Marquis Canova.

Up to this period I never had received any
instructions from a master, nor had I studied in any
academy. At my own request Canova allowed me
to copy his fine Pugilist, the marble statue is in the
Vatican. I began to model my copy from the cast
at the studio. After I had worked at the clay a
few days down it all fell. It seems that my
Master had observed to his foreman, Signor Desti,
that my figure must fall, " for," said he, " you see
that he does not know anything about the skeleton-
work ; but let him proceed. and when his figure
comes down show him how the mechanical part is
done." So when my model fell, a Blacksmith was

called, and the iron work made, and numerous crosses of wood and wire. Such a thing I had never yet seen One of his pupils then put up the clay upon the iron skeleton and roughed out the model before me, so that the figure was as firm as a rock. I was enchanted, and worked a long time upon my copy. One day an English party, consisting of a gentleman and some ladies and a pert little boy, came through the rooms, they stopped a little and looked at my work, they did not speak, but the boy said, " Pa, this fellow can't be very clever, look at the difference of his figure and the big one." I took no notice and they must have thought that I was an Italian.

I finished the copy to the great satisfaction of my master, who said to me that he considered me prepared to go and model at the Academy from the life. There was the Academy of St. Luke, and there was then Canova's academy—he only admitted those that were first-rate, and there were students from different parts of Italy—he put me among the latter. Canova attended these twice a week to overlook and to correct the students. The expenses of this school were defrayed by the Emperor of Austria, but Canova did not receive anything for his attendance.

My master accompanied me to his academy, and there was then sitting as a model a youth of extraordinary beauty ; he was sitting in a very graceful

attitude. When his time of rest came. Canova
said to him, " Alzatevi." The youth sprang up in
a moment, and then Canova said, " l'Apollo
Belvedere." The fellow instantly put himself into
the action of the Apollo and with the utmost
exactness—the lofty air, a touch of ire on the
expression of the face, the swelling nostrils, and
the mouth slightly conveying a feeling of disdain
rendered both the action and expression perfect.
I was delighted, and spoke out my surprise at the
beauty of the young man and his knowledge of
action, expression, and grace; he was like the
statue come to life. Canova believed that a
more beautiful youth could not be found in
Europe. My master again cried " Il Mercurio";
in a moment he was in the spirited attitude of
the Mercury of Giovanni di Bologna. Then the
youth, of his own accord, put himself in the
position of some of Canova's own beautiful statues.

I began modelling from the life, and my Master
advised me to look often at the productions of all
the students there, from the first beginning to the
end—" they will allow you to look over their
models " I did so, and most improving it was to
me. They were all very polite, and expressed
their regret that I did not understand Italian.
When I observed their masterly manner of sketch-
ing in the figure, and the excellent imitation of
nature—the power and experience testified by

youths much younger than myself, caused my
spirits to drop considerably, and I was humbled
and unhappy. How I regretted that I had not
been able to come to Rome much earlier in life!
In this melancholy mood, when I returned at night
to my lonely lodgings, no one to speak to, I sighed
deeply and my gloomy thoughts flew to the past—
and those happy evenings of the readings with all
their pleasing associations, the books, the drawings,
the quiet tea-table, the arranged flowers—the burn-
ing incense, and the graceful presence of my charming and beautiful friend. The first letter which I
received at Rome began—" Oh, come back as soon
as you can, do not delay a moment beyond the
time. I feel as if I had lost a part of myself—
something that belongs to me, when I am no more
there will not remain on Earth any one so imbued
with my nature, my sentiments and my disposition.
There is something so pure and beautiful in what
has connected us that my soul disdains the conceal-
ment of it. You have felt for me more than the
tenderness we do for mothers. My happy star in
some respects brightened your path and called
forth your nature. I like your expression respecting my handwriting ' the sacred hand '—may it be
the first to greet you on your entrance into Rome
and may it always softly remind you of all that
binds us to each other."

I attended the Academy of Canova for three

CUPID AND PSYCHE.

years, every night, and Canova sometimes would
tap me on the shoulder and say: "Bravo, you
are never absent." During the first part of my
practice he observed that I understood anatomy,
but added, "As you improve in imitating nature
you will blend anatomy more, rendering it less
distinct." After three years this Academy was
broken up, for the Emperor stopped the money
which supported it. Those evening studies for
that space of time furthered my progress in no
small degree.

My master then gave me to understand that the
sooner I began to model a figure of my own invention, life-size, from nature, the better, and that I
should take a studio. His foreman found me one
near to his own, that he might have me always
under his own eye.

Among the clay sketches which I had been
composing was one of a sleeping boy, which
Canova said I might execute life-size; he often
came to correct me as it advanced, and his remarks
were of course most invaluable to me. The sleeping shepherd was finished, and I had copied nature
pretty close, as the subject admitted the imitation
of individual nature.

I soon began to be haunted with the idea of
attempting a higher subject. I showed to my
master clay sketches of several groups, but he
advised me to keep to a single figure until I had

more knowledge of style, and experience in form.
I made, however, a small model of Mars and
Cupid, which he approved of, and said that I might
model it on a large scale.   His advice to me was,
to take care not to imitate his style, nor to study
his works too much ; he added, " the best counsel
I can give you is to copy nature, but at the same
time you are working from the life, go constantly
and look at the antique ; not to model copies from
any of the statues, but always to examine them,
and that carefully, until you have gained a perfect
knowledge of their principles, and are aware of all
their perfection."   He also added that I must go
often to the studios of the sculptors around me ;
all their studios being open, " but," he said, " first
of all go as frequently as you can to Thorwaldsen ;
he is a very great artist."

In a letter which I wrote to Mr. Roscoe, dated
May 1818, I said, "I shall see more, I shall do
more, and I shall write more said I to myself; and
thus time flies away without my addressing my
earliest friend.   Now I have not forgotten the
pathways that lead to Allerton.   I have not forgotten your early attentions to me, and which
brought me to the notice of those friends whose
generosity has opened the gates of Rome to me.

" Yes, here I am, and could be contented for
ever in Rome, for I like it more and more.   I have
not yet seen the third part of what this city contains,

for I began to work soon after my arrival here, anxious to show Canova something I have been designing and modelling. A present I have in hand the model of a shepherd-boy sleeping (my own design), which I have been studying from nature. The Marquis was so good as to come to my studio to see it, and he seems much pleased with it. He says that I have made the body and the head beautifully."

‑

CHAPTER V

DUKE OF DEVONSHIRE'S VISIT—MARS AND CUPID—
SIR GEORGE BEAUMONT'S VISIT—PSYCHE AND THE
ZEPHYRS—DEATH OF CANOVA

In the year 1819 I began to model my group of
Mars and Cupid, seven feet high, and worked upon
it with great spirit, having fine living models before
me.   I went to contemplate the Greek statues,
and often drew outlines from them in order to
learn the beauty and delicacy of their lines, also
drawing legs, arms, and torsos separately and
rather large.   I worked many months at my ' Mars
and Cupid,' and when it was very much advanced,
one day I heard knocking at my door. I opened it,
and in came a tall fine-looking young man, and he
said, " The Duke of Devonshire, Canova sent me
to see what you are doing."   I felt a little confused,
and when I was calmed down I got on well with
His Grace.   After examining Mars for some time
he asked me what might be the cost of it in
marble.   I said that, not having experience, I
could not tell.   " Think," said he, " and tell me."

After pondering a little I ventured to say, " Five hundred pounds—perhaps I have said too much." "Oh no, not too much," said His Grace. Before he left the studio, he told me that he would have the group done in marble at the price named I was surprised and much delighted. I soon ran to Canova, and told him of the Duke's visit, and that he had ordered the group in marble : my master was greatly pleased. When I named the price which I had mentioned at random to the Duke, Canova said that he was sorry that I did not propose to consult him upon that subject; he considered that the expense of marble and workmanship would cost at least five hundred pounds. When the group was completed in marble, it cost me five hundred and twenty pounds. I spent nine months upon the clay model, also some months in finishing the marble My group of ' Mars and Cupid ' is at Chatsworth and it was the first commission which I received at Rome.

At that period Sir F. Chantrey came to Rome Canova mentioned me to him, and he came to my little studio in the Via Fontanella. He asked me how long I had been in Rome. I said, " Three years," and that I hoped to remain another three years He then observed, " One three years is enough to spoil you, or any other artist." I said to him, " Did he think I was in a bad school ? " but he made no further reply. Sir F. Chantrey was a man of no genius, he had not received from nature the power of invention, nor had he been trained in early life in the higher department of the art. He devoted himself to the making of busts, and succeeded greatly in those of men, but not equally in those of women. The latter wanted elegance and grace.

On the 13th of October, 1822, the great and good Canova died at Venice; many were those who suffered by his loss; to the needy students he liberally gave money, and to all, valuable instruction. I received constant lessons from him for five years.

In the beginning of this year I began to model my group of Psyche and Zephyrs which my Master had encouraged me to execute. In the winter of that year Sir George Beaumont came to Rome; at that time my clay group was much advanced and Canova sent Sir George to see it. The old gentleman came and returned again frequently. At length he asked me what would be the price of the group in marble. I said that I would put a moderate price and let him know. The next time he came to my studio I was prepared. and named the price of seven hundred pounds; he then ordered the group in marble, to my great delight.

Canova and Sir George sent most of the great people then in Rome to see the group Sir George

PSYCHE BORNE BY THE ZEPHYRS.

and Lady Beaumont often invited me to their house and so did many of the great English people then at Rome.

The Duke of Devonshire returned to Rome that winter and came to see the group on which I was employed and greatly admired it. The 'Mars and Cupid' was still unfinished in my studio. I have already mentioned that whilst at Liverpool I had made a drawing of the meeting of Hero and Leander which I presented to Mrs. Robinson His Grace was much struck with it, and told me that Canova had spoken of it to him, so he ordered it in marble and it is at Chatsworth.

I was much elated by the commission I then received from Sir George Beaumont, one of the first judges of art in England. He did not think, like Sir F. Chantrey, that Rome would spoil me. No! Rome, above all other cities, has a peculiar influence upon, and charm for, the real student, he finds himself actually in the University of Art, where it is the principal subject both of thought and conversation. Constantly did I feel the presence of this influence. Every morning I rose up with the sun, my soul gladdened by a new day of happy and delightful pursuit. As I walked to my breakfast every morning to the Caffé Greco and watched with renewed pleasure the tops of the Churches and Palaces gilt by the rising sun, I felt myself inspired with a feeling of daily renovated youth

and fresh enthusiasm.   How joyfully did I return
to the combat, to that invigorating strife with the
difficulties of art!   Nor did I feel the worm of envy
creeping round my heart whenever I saw in the
studios of others a beautiful idea skilfully executed
by any of my young rivals   I might at times feel a
depression of mind. something like discouragement,
but nothing of that low jealousy; constantly spurred
on by the talents around me I returned to my
studio with fresh resolution.

I had been some time intending to make a
statue of that very finely formed youth of the
Academy to whom I have alluded, and decided to
make a statue of Paris from him, so I began the
model life-size, after I had studied in Rome for two
years.   Mr. W. Taylor, hearing of my progress in
Rome, ordered the Paris of me.

During the progress of the group for Sir George
Beaumont, he occasionally wrote to me.   In a
letter from Berne, July 1st, 1822, he says—" I
request you will send a letter to me to Geneva,
to inform me of your progress—whether you have
got the marble.   You will easily imagine I am
extremely anxious to know how you go on.

" When you see the Marquis Canova pray
present our affectionate regards to him, tell him I
shall never forget his kind attentions, and that I
can most sincerely assure him if all we had gained
by our journey to Rome had been the acquisition

of his acquaintance, I hope I may say, friendship, we should think our trouble amply repaid, in short, as Lady Beaumont has already told him, we love as much as we admire him."

In a letter dated Paris, August 28th, 1822, there is the following:—"When I was at Lausanne I passed an hour with my very old friend John Kemble; he spoke of you with great regard and mentioned the bust you made of him at Liverpool, and was very much pleased to hear how you were about to be employed. Mr. and Mrs. Kemble mean to pass the winter at Rome—he must be esteemed and admired wherever he goes, and I almost envy the pleasure you will enjoy, to see him in his Toga at the Vatican, how much he will be at home among the Brutuses, the Cæsars and the Pompeys, and how much he will look like one of their party.

"My imagination figures to me the state of your marble at present, and I almost flatter myself that the work is so far advanced that one might trace the general subject—you will, I know, lose no time, yet I would by no means hurry you, or induce you to injure your health, by over application, especially whilst the hot weather continues.

"I thank you again and again for your attention to my letters, though your kindness has been unnecessarily interfered with—every good wish of ours attend you, you are enjoying fair Italy, the true soil in which all the arts shine—may you enjoy health also, to practice and improve in an art for which you are so admirably qualified—in this Lady Beaumont cordially joins."

"COLE ORTON HALL,
"Ashby de la Zouch,
"*August* 24*th*, 1823.

"MY DEAR SIR,

"I confess I should have written to you before this time, but I can assure you, I am not less interested in your proceedings, both for others and myself, than if I had troubled you with a letter every post. Neither have I the least doubt of your diligence and ultimate success—in every way you have my best and kindest wishes. I saw Mr. Sneyd on his return, before I left London, and he gave me very satisfactory accounts of the state of the group —satisfactory I say, because it always gave me pleasure to hear of your success, although I never doubted it. The liberal patronage of the Duke of Devonshire does him the highest honour, and gives general satisfaction, and I need not say how much his attention to you pleases me in particular.

"Canova's Endymion arrived a few days before I quitted London and was universally admired. I almost think it the finest work of our great and excellent friend. This is difficult to decide, but at any rate I think we may say none of his other works can exceed it. I saw and examined it by

day and by night, and I hardly decide by which
light it appears to the greatest advantage. You
know how jealous we are, almost to prudery, of all
superfluous ornament, but assuredly the most
fastidious taste can find no fault with the
Endymion—nothing can be more pure and the
distinction between sleep and death is perfect—it
perfectly breathes—I fancy him to be dreaming of
Diana, and there is a gentle action of the feet
which seems to foretell he will soon awake, and
accounts for the spirited action of the dog, who
evidently expects the event. It roused all my
enthusiasm, my admiration and my grief for the
loss of the excellent author."

"GROSVENOR SQUARE,
"*May* 10*th*, 1824.

"MY DEAR SIR,

"I feel myself much to blame for having so
long neglected to write, and I hope you will excuse
me. Your account of the progress you have made
in the group is highly gratifying, and your
energetic expressions respecting the pains you have
taken and the exertions you are resolved to make,
do you the highest honour and would have satisfied
me if I had not been previously convinced, that
you are in the right road to excellence, and I feel
confident you will never deviate, but press forward
until you obtain every honour which your noble

art has in its power to confer. The liberal conduct of the Duke of Devonshire in wishing you to proceed without interruption in the work you had begun for me, is of a piece with all he does, and adds to his character as a noble and judicious patron, and I have no doubt posterity will consider him as the most splendid encourager of the arts which this age has produced.

"I have to thank you greatly for the medal and the hand of our admired friend Canova. I cannot express my feelings, when I took hold of the latter; it reminded me strongly of the last grasp I received from the living hand, after he had taken the trouble, tho' very ill, of going over the Vatican with Lady Beaumont and myself. It was a pressure, warm from the heart, and affected me greatly, and when I looked up, and saw the languor of his countenance, I felt a sad foreboding, which was too soon realized. He departed the next morning for Naples, and I never saw him more. I believe no death was ever more generally and deeply lamented. I do not believe he had an enemy in the world. or harboured a feeling towards any human creature inconsistent with the purest Christian charity.

"I cannot promise myself a sight of Rome and its inexhaustible treasures this year, indeed, I feel the weight of years creeping upon me; consider this and let me have your excellent work, for I know it will be inestimable to me, as soon as you can. I cannot but think this kind consideration weighed with the Duke when he so generously preferred you to proceed with the Psyche."

In another letter from Sir George dated January 1st, 1827, there is the following:—" We had the pleasure, a few weeks ago, of a visit from the venerable Mrs. Siddons, and altho' time has certainly produced a change, yet he has done it with so respectful and gentle a hand that the upper part of her fine face retains all the majesty of her middle age, insomuch that I verily believe she could perform characters suited to her years with all her primeval power. We talked much of you and she expressed her opinion of your talents in a manner you would not have been displeased at. This is the beginning of 1827—the beginning of another year is a serious undertaking at my time of life—I sincerely wish you many times the return of this day, and that each succeeding year may find you increasing in reputation and virtue—for Glory will not confer happiness without it—of this the great M Angelo was fully sensible, and has feelingly expressed it in the sonnet[1] in which he begins—

'Now is the voyage nearly overpast
And my frail bark,' etc

---

[1] Rime. Sonnet CXIX
Giunto è già 'l corso della vita mia,
Con tempesto mar per fragil barca,

I daresay you know it, and it is a striking thing when such a great and successful man seems sensible of the comparative littleness of all that ' Man pursues below.' Yet it never impaired his energy, therefore I wish you to feel it in the same way."

In the year 1824 Lord George Cavendish came to Rome, and the Duke of Devonshire was the cause of his Lordship visiting my Studio. He admired the sleeping Shepherd-boy which I had modelled, and gave me an order to execute it in marble for him.

I find by a letter from Lord George Cavendish, that this statue arrived in London in November 1825. His lordship says: " I have been lately so much engaged that I have not been able sooner to acquaint you of the safe arrival of the Shepherd-boy. It has been unpacked, and placed on a temporary pedestal by Mr. Chantrey's people. All who have seen it admire it exceedingly."

Al cumun porto, ov'a render si varca,
  Giusta ragion d'ogn' opra trista, a pia.
Onde l'affetuosa fantasia,
  Che l'arta si fece idolo e monarca,
  Conosco ben quant' d'error carca ;
  Ch'errore è ciò che l'huom quaggiù desia
I pensier miei già de me' danni lieti,
  Che fian' or s'a due morti m'avvicino
  L'una m'e certa, el 'altra mi munaccia.
  Ne pingei, nes colpu fia più che queti,
  L'anima volta a quell' amor divina,
  Ch apeise a prendei noi in croce le braccia

The progress of my Paris for Mr. W. Taylor was delayed on account of the block turning out defective. I began it over again, having procured a new piece of marble, and here is a part of one of Mr. W. Taylor's letters dated Nov., 1824. "If, however. this new Carrara block should fail you, when somewhat advanced, proceed, and let me have it as it may turn out—should the material be defective I am sure there will be no defect in the workmanship which the energy of your mind, your proficiency, and the correctness of your feelings can guard you against—so I shall expect, and welcome with sincere pleasure, the work and the Artist.

" If you had living children, be assured, you would feel for them much as you do for those created by your imagination and your chisel. The same trains of feeling direct the heart and the imagination in one case as in the other. For my four sons Simon, John, George (our third), and Emilius, and my very pretty daughter, I have all those parental anxieties which you so well describe as entertained by you for your marble progeny, and I shall have as much pleasure and pride in presenting them to you, when you make your promised visit to us, as you will have when you present to us your oldest son, Paris, for I shall always designate him as your first work because it was so designed, and partially executed. The will for the deed is in this case admissible.

"Mrs. W Taylor and our children and myself are in perfect health—we are proceeding in the enlargement and embellishment of our House and Place in Wilts, where we shall be really happy to welcome you, and where your Paris will find himself in very good company."

He writes on the 4th November, 1826:

"I was beginning a complaint against you of forgetfulness of an old friend, when Mr. MacArthur returned from Rome, who has given so very satisfactory a report to me of yourself, of your feelings, of your exertions, and of your progress towards the completion of my Paris that I have now only to express the sincere pleasure I shall experience in welcoming him to this country, and yourself also whenever you may be disposed to quit the seat of your success for that Cradle of your genius, short as, I presume, the visit will be. Mr. MacArthur considers your work amongst the first, if not indeed the first, of the efforts of modern sculpture, and I trust that the connoisseurs here will agree with him. We shall all be very glad to see you—I hear much good of you. Let Paris remain nude—Mrs. Taylor has no false delicacy."

And again he writes: "By the death of Flaxman and the quietude of Chantrey, who has made a considerable fortune, there is a great opening in the line of sculpture at present in this country. Mr. Seguier made this observation to me with reference to yourself—but you must be the best judge whether Gibson of Rome or Gibson of London would be likely to be the most considerable personage."

I had at this period been ten years at Rome. I felt that by my progress in the race which I was running I had left some of my young rivals (Italians) behind me. As I advanced, my ambition for fame became stronger and stronger—"go to London"—thought I—" no—what is local Fame? If I live, I will try for universal celebrity. I may fail—yes—but Rome shall be my battlefield where I shall be surrounded by more powerful antagonists than are to be found in England—there my life would be spent in making busts and statues of great men in anti-sculptural dress. Here I am with many others employed upon poetical subjects—those that demand the highest efforts of the imagination and the greatest knowledge of the beautiful. How often have my countrymen observed to me that in England I should become a rich man; my reply has always been that I have no use for wealth since my wants are very few in this world, and my greatest happiness is the study of my art."

CHAPTER VI

SIR WATKIN W WYNN'S VISIT TO ROME—ENGLISH
OPINION OF HIS WORKS—ELECTED A MEMBER OF
ST LUKE'S ACADEMY—DEATH OF MRS ROBINSON—
THE CONCEPTION OF EROS

In May 1826 Mr. Haldiman came to Rome, and
when he came to my studio I was modelling a
group of three figures representing the youth Hylas
surprised at the fountain by the nymphs—he
seemed fascinated with the model, and before he
left Rome he honoured me by ordering it in
marble. Mr. Haldiman afterwards changed his
residence from England and went to live at Geneva
for the remainder of his life. From the latter
place he wrote to me at Rome requesting, on very
liberal terms, to be allowed to relinquish the group
he had ordered of me. I sold it afterwards to the
late Mr. Vernon, whose collection has now become
public property by his bequest to the nation.

In the winter of the same year, the late Sir
Watkin Williams Wynn came to Rome. Having
heard that I was a native of Conway he made up his

HYLAS SURPRISED BY THE NAIADES.

[To face p. 98.

mind that I should execute a work for him and that it should be the statue of an eagle in marble. I felt discouraged at the proposal of such a subject, and at this moment there stood before us my group of Psyche and Zephyrs. He expressed his admiration of it, but what could I think of his admiration when he said, "If you take away the Psyche and put in her place a time-piece, it will make a capital clock?"

When I saw Sir Watkin beginning to change my composition according to his own ideas I lost all hopes of him. He said, "Then you don't care about doing an eagle for me?" I said, "No, Sir Watkin, that is out of my way." I then directed his attention to a figure of Cupid I was modelling drawing an arrow with one hand, and holding his bow with the other. He immediately asked me "Would you like to do that for me in marble?" I then said that I should be delighted, and then he replied, "Well, well, then do it"—so my statue of Cupid was executed in marble for him. The old gentleman was exceedingly kind to me during his stay in Rome, and also his sister, Miss Williams Wynn. Sir Watkin, on account of his extreme amiability was a favourite with everybody in Rome.

On May the 12th, 1826, I had the honour of being elected an honorary member of the Pontifical Academy of Bologna.

In the year 1827 my group of Psyche and

Zephyrs was exhibited in the Royal Academy Exhibition after the death of Sir George Beaumont, who died in the country without seeing it.

Judging from the tone of the press respecting my first work, which I had sent from Rome, it was evident that my group caused alarm in the camp of my competitors. It was already known that my work was ordered by one of the greatest judges on art in England, and it was well known too that the Duke of Devonshire had previously honoured me with his patronage. The group was said to be inferior to the performances produced at home. One of the articles in the daily papers asserted that its only merit consisted in the beautiful finish of the material. The same paper contained a long eulogium upon a figure of some gentleman by Chantrey. I will here give another letter of Mr. W. Taylor.

"EARLESTOKE PARK,
"30th December, 1828.

"You must indeed think me a strange neglectful person, for not having immediately thanked you upon the safe arrival of Paris. But in truth altho' I did not write, I have been anything but inattentive to your interest, or insensible to your kindness in the successful exertions you have made to render Paris worthy of yourself and most acceptable to us. I delayed from day to day writing.

under the expectation of having to communicate
to you the judgment of more important connoisseurs
than ourselves here upon your work, and I have
now that great satisfaction. I considered it more
conducive to your professional reputation that Paris
should be seen and admired at this place—standing
(as he does) in a distinguished station in a very
handsome spacious apartment rather than in being
mixed with other works in the dark, little, crowded
room at Somerset House, with all that envy, ill-
nature and prejudice could deal out unjustly and
shabbily upon it. As an absentee at Rome you are
considered by a certain set, who can give a cry
one way or another, an alien Competitor, and the
John Bull feeling in favour of native talent last
year certainly was stirred up to pronounce upon
your group of Psyche and Zephyrs as inferior to
works which were notoriously not equal to yours."

It will be seen by this letter that Mr. W. Taylor
very justly considered that my work would be
shown to more advantage and less exposed to
malicious misrepresentation if exhibited in his
Mansion rather than in the show-room of the Royal
Academy, and he further adds—" In a private
collection, a dispassionate judgment may be (and
generally will be) passed upon works of art, and
such has been the case with your Paris All the
general visitors to this place have concurred in the

sentiment of just admiration of it, but I more
particularly notify to you that Lord Farnborough
has seen it here, and pronounced it to be one of the
finest efforts of modern art that he had seen, and
was certainly struck with it particularly.   The
influence his lordship has with the King made me
very desirous that he should see it to the best
advantage, and that has been the case, as Lady
Farnborough and his Lordship, with Mr Seguier,
Mr. Jackson (the artist), Mr. Stanfield (a most
rising artist) passed a week with us, and all concurred
in approbation of your Paris.   As Mr. Seguier
(who was warm in its praise) is now entirely
engaged in the King's service, arranging the R.
collection at Windsor, and has frequent opportunities of seeing H.M., and in the most confidential
favour with Lord F., I shall try at a proper
opportunity to set them on to suggest to H.M. the
merits of Paris, with the hope that H M. might
be induced to wish for some specimen of your
skill—but H.M. is now so difficult of access, that
such a sentiment may not be struck out.   As to
H.M. seeing Paris, that was out of the question, as
he has now given up going to the British Gallery
or any other place, and all works of art are carried
to St. James's or to Windsor for his inspection in
private.   Now Paris is too heavy a gentleman to
pay the British Priam a visit.   Jackson (who
travelled with Chantrey to Rome and took Canova's

portrait) pronounced that your Paris was more true
to nature than Canova would have rendered it.
He is dry in his remarks and meant no strained
compliment. I will not trouble you with the
various remarks made, as you can anticipate most
of them—I will merely say that the character of
the countenance, the ease of the position, the
torso, the right knee, the hands, etc., have been particularly admired as well as the delicate, yet decided
marking of the youthful muscles, looking from
the left in front; one or two uninitiated observers
have questioned whether the retiring of the right
arm does not give a constrained appearance to the
figure. But the necessity for that position of the
arm and the expression of deliberation which it
conveys give an immediate answer to such criticisms.
In short, you have every reason to be satisfied with
the reception which Paris has hitherto experienced,
and which from time to time will be improved upon
as future visitors of taste repair to our residence."

In the year 1829 Baron Cammuccini, the historical
painter, suggested to Thorwaldsen to propose me
at a meeting of the Academicians of St. Luke's
to elect me a member; at that time the sculptor
Massimiliano died, and his place was to be filled up.
Thorwaldsen and the Baron, with others, worked
hard to have me chosen in his room. The white
balls were more numerous than the black ones, and
I was elected Resident Academician of Merit.

When this honour was conferred upon me I had studied in Rome twelve years.

In the year 1829 I lost my friend Mrs. Robinson, and with the permission of her sister, Mrs. Lawrence of Liverpool, I executed and erected a small monument to her memory, representing her in a sitting attitude with an upward look, and a book in her hand. There I have endeavoured to give her beautiful Greek profile. The memorial is placed in the little chapel of the cemetery at Liverpool.

The following letter is from Mr. Roscoe:—" I avail myself of the opportunity of Mr. and Mrs. Gaskell's visiting Rome to thank you for the many instances of your kindness and friendship I have lately received, particularly for the great honour you have done me in presenting my Bust to the Liverpool Royal Institution and the letter to the Secretary, Mr. Martin, by which it was introduced —a letter which by some means, but without my knowledge, found its way into the public papers and was thought no less honourable to your own feelings than to the character which you were pleased to express of me, and with which (if I could but flatter myself with having deserved it) I should be so highly gratified. The Bust arrived a few weeks since in perfect safety, and altho' from the state of my health I have seen of late but little company, I have frequently heard it spoken of with high commendation.

"The cast of your charming group of Psyche and Zephyrs occupies a central station in our collection of statuary, where it forms a principal ornament, and is seen with universal admiration

"The death of Sir George Beaumont, with whom I was of late years acquainted, gave me the sincerest sorrow, and his letter to you, which you were so kind as to copy for me, whilst it increased my esteem for him, added to my affliction.

"I hope it will not be long before the *Amor Patriæ* will induce you to pay a visit to your native country, even though you should think proper to return again to Rome. In this case no one will be more happy to see you again, attended by that celebrity which your own genius and talents have acquired, than,

"My dear Sir

"Your truly affectionate and faithful friend,

"W. Roscoe."

Lord George Cavendish, having shown my statue of the Sleeping Shepherd to Lord Yarborough, wrote to inform me that his friend wished to have a work by me, some graceful female statue At that time I was modelling a figure of a nymph sitting, and whilst arranging her sandal, her attention is drawn off, which gives a momentary suspense to her occupation. Her form is slender and very youthful. I enclosed a slight outline of it

in a letter to Lord George that he might shew it to
his friend, the result was that Lord Yarborough
ordered it to be executed for him in marble.
I received this commission in the year 1824. I
had the nymph in hand six years, owing to my
various occupations. I received the following
letter from Lord Yarborough, on receiving the
statue.

"ARLINGTON STREET,
    "2nd November, 1830.

" I have the satisfaction of informing you your
statue is safely deposited in my house in London,
and I assure you I have been viewing your work
with very great delight. The more I inspect, I
approve of your taste, the whole figure is so beautifully worked, and really the pretty young modest
girl I think perfection. I expect Lord George
Cavendish in town daily. I am quite sure he will
be delighted with the statue. Lord George informed me of your request that your statue should
be exhibited next spring, I assure you I shall have
great pleasure in sending it. '

My nymph was placed at the Academy Exhibition of that year.

In the same year Mrs. Dudley North, sister to
Lord Yarborough, came to Rome with a letter from
Lord George Cavendish to me; she intended to
raise a statue to the memory of her husband, the

late Dudley North. After she saw all my works, she
gave me the order to execute the monumental
statue of her deceased husband ; she had brought
with her a cast of the likeness modelled by
Nollekens, so I had no difficulty about the likeness.
I modelled the figure sitting in a chair. The
statue was lost at sea, but it was insured, and Mrs.
Dudley North wrote to me to reproduce the work,
which I did. In the same year I modelled a statue
of Flora, and it was ordered by Lord Durham.

On taking up the Aminta of Tasso, we read in
the Prologue [1]—

> " Chi crederia che sotto umane forme
> E sotto queste pastorali spoghe
> Fosse nascosto un Dio? non mica un Dio
> Selvaggio, o della plebe degli Dei,
> Ma tra grandi Celesti il piu possente
> Che fa spesso cader di mano a Marte
> La sanguinosa spada, ed a Nettuno,
> Scotitor della terra, il gran tridente,
> E le folgori eterne al sommo Giove
> In quest' aspetto, certo, e in questi panni
> Non riconoscerà Si di leggiero
> Venere madre me suo figlio, Amore "

I modelled Love disguised as a shepherd, attired
in a short cloak and hat The potent God of Love
slily concealing behind him the heart-piercing dart,
he seeks to inspire confidence by advancing his
right hand towards you, and assumes that air of
modesty and timidity to conceal the more his
cunning designs; behind, below the edge of his

[1] The opening lines.

mantle, are just seen the points of his folded
wings.

As I dwelt upon the spirit of my subject, as I
sat meditating before my new production and
longing after perfection, that pure divine beauty
which enchants the soul, my imagination, began to
soar up to the God himself—" Oh Eros, canst thou
disguise thy celestial countenance, or conceal thy
ambrosial locks which wave luxuriantly round thy
feminine shoulders? Thy little hands are too
delicate for a shepherd, and so are those lovely
limbs—will not thy god-like steps betray thee?
Tell me, God of Beauty and Love, is this image,
this humble mortal effort, in some degree tolerable
in thy sight?" " I approve," said the God, " but
do not leave it white, it chills me! Zeus is well
aware of the fiery glance of my eyes, here, my
figure appears stone blind, I cannot tolerate such a
sacrifice. When the Graces tie up my little top-
knot, which they, as well as my mother, always
make me wear, they will never suffer those white
locks. When Praxiteles finished my statue in
marble the one with gold wings which he gave to
his beautiful Phryne, and which she dedicated at
Thespiae, he called Nicias to give it the last finish,
that is, my own complexion, not that of a mortal,
for we Gods feed upon ambrosia and drink nectar
from the hands of Hebe, therefore give me my
celestial glow, warm, pale, and pure. Often have I

CUPID PURSUING PSYCHE.

been represented in marble with 'parti-coloured wings and my quiver painted in the usual fashion.' No sculptor should presume to represent me without being aware of the peculiarity of my nature and form, which is androgynous, the passion of love which my power inspires being equally divided between the two sexes. All this has been revealed to mortals in the Orphic doctrines. I have now been absent a long while from my Mother, she is alarmed for me, and has offered a reward of a kiss to any one who can find me. but I will keep her waiting still longer for I have promised to meet Ganymede in the gardens of Zeus and play at osselets, also to exercise myself a little with my golden sphaerae. My mother never can remain long without me, for in my absence she is powerless, it is my arrows that carry her will as quick as thought wherever she wishes. She is also dependent upon her constant companion Peitho, for Persuasion never leaves Aphrodite. Here come my celestial relations Pothos and Imeros accompanied by the three amiable Charities, but I do not see the graceful Hymenaeus, he must be presiding at a marriage. How the air is perfumed as they approach! Cover, cover up that cold white Statue of me, for they will not bear the sight of anything so chilly, repulsive, and contrary to reason." " Is it permitted, oh Divine Eros, to know why your Brothers keep their golden locks like

virgins and their beautiful ankles adorned with
gold rings?" "They are," said the God, "like
myself, androgynous. I must now render myself
invisible to the Charities for I suspect Aphrodite
has sent them in search of me, but I will not return
to her yet awhile—she may increase her reward for
me to more kisses than one.'

My statue of Cupid disguised as a shepherd was
exhibited at the Royal Academy Exhibition, but he
made no impression upon the hearts of the daily
paper critics. The statue was executed in marble
for Sir John Johnstone, and repeated for Sir Robert
Peel, for the Hereditary Grand Duke of Russia
(now Emperor), Mr. Collins Wood, and Lord
Crewe, also for Mr. Appleton of Boston, Mr.
Farnham of Philadelphia; altogether it was repeated
in marble seven times. I believe the idea was new
in sculpture as I have not seen it.

In the year 1831 I modelled a group of Venus
kissing Cupid. Lord Yarborough having written to
me to know if I had any new subject in hand, I
enclosed to him a drawing of my new group. The
idea pleased him much, and he ordered me to do it
in marble for him. It was completed after great
labour, and sent to the Royal Academy Exhibition
by his Lordship at my request.

VENUS AND CUPID

CHAPTER VII

THE HUSKISSON STATUE—THORWALDSEN AND CAMMUC-
CINI—ELECTED A MEMBER OF THE ROYAL ACADEMY
—THE IDEA OF THE WOUNDED AMAZON

AFTER the melancholy death of Mr. Huskisson, it being decided to erect in Liverpool a statue to his memory, artists were invited and I among the rest to send in models for that purpose. Being impressed with the bad results of competition on these occasions and the difficulty which those not connected with art at all have in selecting the best designs, and knowing how the gentlemen on these committees are beset by artists and their friends to obtain the work, I declined competing; the commission was afterwards given to me on my own terms.

In the year 1831 I commenced the clay model which I finished in five months. It made an impression on the best judges at Rome; Mrs. Huskisson hearing of the success of the work, came to Rome on purpose to see it while it was still in clay. After her arrival she soon fixed by appointment a morning to come to the studio.

When the hour arrived I dismissed the men that she might contemplate the model undisturbed—she arrives—I receive her with some agitation—conduct her to the room—she sat before it, looked and looked, and burst into tears, keeping her face covered for some time , after a long death-like silence she said—"You have been most successful"; and again becoming affected she retired with me, saying, that she would return next day. About this time a letter came to me from the committee saying they had been informed that I was modelling the statue of Mr. Huskisson with a bare arm and shoulder. I showed the letter to Mrs. Huskisson, when she was standing again before the model she said, "Oh, I hope that beautiful arm will not be covered!" Soon afterwards she informed me that she had spoken to the Marquis of Anglesea, then in Rome, and he had written to a friend of his who communicated with the committee to allow the statue to remain as I had modelled it; a second letter came to me to tell me to finish the statue without any alteration. It was completed in marble and placed in the new Cemetery in Liverpool within a circular temple by Mr. Foster over the spot where the remains of Mr. Huskisson repose.

I executed a statue of Sappho for the late Mr. Ellams of Allerton Hall near Liverpool; he had purchased Allerton from Mr. Roscoe, and this

THE RT. HON. WILLIAM HUSKISSON.

statue was placed in the room which used to be his library.

About this time I modelled a statue of a youthful female dancer in repose, which Thorwaldsen recommended to the late Count Schonbrun of Bavaria, as a companion to a youthful Faun by Tenerani, the pupil of Thorwaldsen.

It is time for me to acknowledge the great obligations I owe to the late Cavalier Thorwaldsen, he was like Canova, most liberal in his attentions to young artists, visiting all those who solicited his advice. I profited greatly by the knowledge which this splendid artist had of his art. On every occasion when a new work was modelled by me he came to see it, and corrected such errors as were apparent to him. I often went to his studio to contemplate his great and noble works which were always in the noblest style of art, so full of pure, severe simplicity. His power of invention was prolific, numerous were the subjects which he treated, profane and sacred. His studio was a safe school for the young and his precepts directed them to the only true road to the sublime in sculpture. His studio was the resort of artists and lovers of art from all nations. The old man's person never can be forgotten by those who have seen him. Tall and strong, never lost a tooth in his life, he was most venerable-looking with his good-natured

countenance marked by hard-thinking, his eyes
were grey, and his white hair down to his broad
shoulders ; at the great assemblies his breast was
covered with orders.

I also had the advantage of the friendship and
great kindness of the late Baron Cammuccini—
who was the first historical painter in Italy. I
always felt that he would have made a greater
sculptor than a painter, many of his best works
have great power of composition and fine drawing.
He had the most correct judgment and pure taste
in sculpture of any painter I have known. The
sculptors do not allow that painters generally
speaking are perfect judges in their art. At a very
early period Cammuccini began to teach me that
unity of parts which is necessary throughout the
figure ; and this to me was not so easy a matter,
but in the course of time I felt a more acute
perception of that quality which is so perfect in all
the works of the Greeks. He also used to dwell
upon the subject of Grace—true grace never affects
the natural simplicity of action—grace is perfect in
the best models of the antique, it is always there,
but at the same time felt rather than perceived.
The rules of grace are definable, but there is a
feeling of it in the soul, which cannot be taught—
it is a divine gift which ever attends true genius.

One morning early I was taking my usual walk
on the Monte Pinciano, and there was a fountain

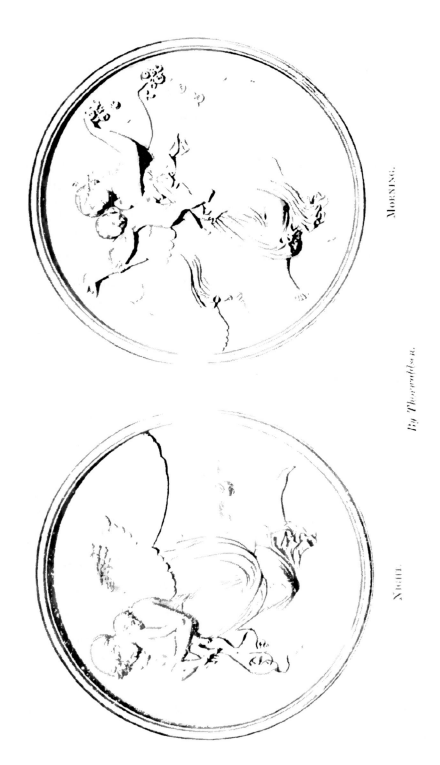

MORNING.

By Thorwaldsen.

NIGHT.

under the wall of the French Academy. I saw a boy sitting on the edge of the fountain with one leg tucked under him looking into the water, his weight was principally sustained by his left arm and leg, the latter being brought under his right thigh The action was perfect for a statue of Narcissus I looked well at him and impressed him upon my memory, immediately went to my studio and modelled a small sketch in clay of the action which I admired. Afterwards I modelled the figure life-size. At that time Lord Barrington came to Rome and visited my studio; after seeing my model several times, he said one day, " I ought not to go to the expense of a statue, but I confess I admire your Narcissus so much I cannot leave Rome without ordering it in marble "; so I executed my Narcissus for Lord Barrington, and it was repeated in marble for Mr. Fort of Manchester, also for Mr. Errington, and I made a repetition and presented it to the Royal Academy after my election; every member must give one of his own works to be placed there. The following part of a letter I received from Lord Barrington : "I must now tell you that Narcissus arrived quite safe. It is without exception one of the most beautiful modern figures in sculpture I ever saw, and I admire it more and more every time I look at it; everybody also who sees it is of the same opinion " (Feb. 23rd, 1833)

G 2

In the year 1834 Sir Robert Peel came to Rome
and he ordered me to make him a repetition
in marble of my statue of Cupid disguised as a
shepherd, and this statue is at Drayton Manor.

Notwithstanding the depreciatory tone of the
London articles on my Anglo-Roman works most
of which were in the possession of persons of
distinction who had visited Rome, I was informed
that there was a feeling in the Academy to elect
me an Associate, provided that I conformed to
their regulations. I consented, and requested my
friend Mr. Eastlake to put down my name as
a candidate. He accordingly informed me by
letter that he had done so.

In the year 1833 I was elected Associate of the
Royal Academy of Arts in London.

I received the following from the Royal
Academy :—

" LONDON.
" 13 *Feby.* 1836.

" Dear Sir

" I have the pleasure to acquaint you that you
were on the 10th inst., in a General Assembly of
the Academicians elected an Academician of the
Royal Academy of Arts of London

("Signed)   HENRY HOWARD, R.A. Sec."

Besides the study of the human forms, the true
and diligent sculptor must attentively watch the

movements of nature, which may casually come under his notice. By such observations he becomes original in his conceptions, and is enabled moreover to represent simple, natural and graceful action in all his works. After impressing these momentary attitudes upon his memory, he must hasten home, and make his sketch on paper. The streets of Rome, in this respect, may afford to the young artist so disposed, an excellent Academy. The inhabitants of warm climates are more free and graceful than those of cold. Nature unconfined by the restrictions of fashion is the true school for the artist.

There the sculptor of the Dying Gladiator first saw his imperishable work. There the boy was seen taking the thorn out of his foot, and it is there, evidently, Praxiteles found his young Faun leaning against the trunk of a tree. The beautiful Discobolus of Naucides and that of Myron; also the Cupid bending his bow, and thus displaying an attitude so often seen in Nature, may likewise be numbered among those statues which were at first presented to the mind of the Artist in all the truthfulness of unpremeditated action. There are many antique repetitions of these beautiful works.

I had frequently noticed women and girls in the streets stopping suddenly and turning round looking backward at their heel and at the same moment drawing their dress a little up. This action is

always most graceful, and one day I made a sketch
in clay, and I was much pleased with the effect,
but day after day I puzzled my brain for a subject
to suit my sketch —all in vain ! Musing on the
subject one day, all of a sudden, the idea of a
wounded Amazon struck me.   Modifying the
attitude, I made my Amazon lifting up the tunic
with her left hand, stooping a little to look at the
wound she has received upon the outside of her
thigh.   With the right-hand fingers she touches
the wound , her heel being raised up, is supported
by the toes which still touch the ground.   This
attitude is most natural and perfectly suited to
what she is doing.   Thus came forth one of my
most esteemed works. and I spent months upon
the clay model.   At that time there lived in Rome
an English gentleman who was considered by
many of our countrymen as a great judge in art,
one day he came to see my model of the Amazon,
and he made a critical remark.   I thanked him, and
said I would consider it.   In a few days he returned, looked at my model hastily and said, " Ha,
I see you have corrected what I pointed out.   I
am glad you think it better   Beautiful," said
he—but I had never touched it.

Before my clay Amazon was finished, Lord
Grosvenor, now the Marquis of Westminster,
came to Rome, and he took an early opportunity
of visiting my studio, and began to admire my

model of the Amazon. His Lordship returned, and ordered the figure in marble. This statue, after more than common labour, was finished and sent to England, and his lordship allowed it to go to the Royal Academy Exhibition, where, as usual, the press did not puff it up, as they did the home performances there. I received the following letter from his lordship :—

" MR. GIBSON,

" I must ask you to accept my excuses for not having written to you before, but I was detained longer than usual this spring in the country, and postponed writing till I had an opportunity of seeing the Amazon in London I was only able to do so two days ago, and am very much pleased with the result of your labours, and approved her much as an interesting classical composition. I am not sure whether the leg is not thrown rather more forward than I should have placed it, but I have no doubt of your correctness.

" May I ask you to make my remembrances to Mr. Williams the painter, and to tell him I hope I shall find my picture advanced when I arrive at Rome.

" 30*th May*, 1840."

The Prince Torlonia had been repairing his Palace, and employing fresco painters, also he was ordering several marble statues from native sculptors. The Prince admired my group of Psyche, carried by Zephyrs, and decided to have it in marble. I accordingly executed a repetition of my group for him in the course of three years, and he was very much satisfied. My group stands at the bottom of the staircase. Prince Torlonia is the only Roman who has ordered works of art at Rome.

CHAPTER VIII

THE PRINCIPLES OF GREEK SCULPTURE—HIS CONCEPTION OF EROS AND PSYCHE

SCULPTURE is the delight of my soul, because it is more elevating than any of the other departments of the arts; its highest aim is the sublime and the purest beauty. To arrive at this lofty degree is the great difficulty. There is only one straight road to perfection and this path has been already pointed out clearly by Winckelmann;[1] the young Sculptor should assiduously study him. The Greeks carried sculpture to the highest possible degree of perfection. Their teacher was Nature alone, under whose guidance they established the standard of beauty, Nature in all her emotions and in all her movements. Their statues are copied from the life

[1] Abbé Winckelmann (1717-1768), a German scholar, who was Prefect of the Vatican Library. He was so struck by the decay of art in Germany and Italy, that he wrote his *History of Art among the Ancients*, a French translation of which was published in 1764, to exhort artists to take their models from Greek art. Another book, *Reflections on the Painting and Sculpture of the Greeks*, was translated into English (Fuseli, 1765). Both books profoundly influenced Gibson, who frequently quotes from them.

89

in all their details, and are by no means conventional, as some have ventured to affirm. These noble performances teach us the Golden Rules by which alone we ought to be guided, if we desire to produce works as imperishable as theirs.

All those men of genius in modern times who have deviated from the principles of Greek art have left us works not superior but greatly inferior to the ancients—we should profit by their errors. The desire of novelty destroys pure taste and some artists neglect the true principles of beauty for the purpose of producing something new and thereby to attract the ignorant Novelty diverts us, truth and perfection instruct us. Thanks to those who have left us works of the novel class, those works have been of no mean service to us inasmuch as they have shown us distinctly what we should avoid. Socrates asserts that "evils have a necessary subsistence, and that it is necessary that there should be something contrary to good" Amongst the artists who, for the sake of novelty, have deviated from the true principles of Greek art, we may number M. Angelo and Bernini and his followers The former is universally and justly acknowledged to have been a mighty genius and the latter possessed great talent. But it is to be regretted that there should be an entire absence of the simplicity of nature, and the refined beauty of form, the easy grace, and the sedate grandeur by

which the works of the Ancient masters are so pre-
eminently distinguished. It is the love of novelty
which leads men astray. The Greeks were not
impeded in their pursuit of perfection by any vain
desire of that kind; they steadily advanced to
the pattern of perfection which nature presented
to them. The Greek artists were companions
of philosophers. Winckelmann is our modern guide
in sculpture, but the attempts to produce something new have frequently led artists away from
the path which Winckelmann has pointed out in his
most valuable work.

Knowledge of beauty and the judgment in
appreciating it, are the first endowments which the
sculptor must possess. Beauty, which has a positive
existence in creation, whatever may be said to the
contrary, would present her charms in vain to the
artist unless he had the power of selecting and
combining those parts that approach nearest to
perfection from those which happen to be less
beautiful for the purpose of forming thereby one
harmonious whole. This union of the beauties
which are dispersed in nature, produces the most
refined forms which the mind can possibly conceive.
To see the human figure represented in the abstract,
animated by expression, moving or at rest, fills the
imagination with delight, and we feel elevated,
exalted by the idea of such perfection: these are
the feelings which the Apollo of Belvedere inspires:

that divine statue is a mighty effort of the human mind. I never can look at that work without feeling new admiration and wonder.

The abstract principles of Art were suggested to the minds of the Greeks by the peculiarities of their religious system.   It was necessary that the images of the Gods must be more beautiful than those of man, also greater in size, magnitude, beauty, and severe simplicity ; always impress the spectator with admiration and awe. It may be said, "yes, all this we know already ; " but I should reply when we see so many wandering from the right path, what I have stated cannot be too often proclaimed.

Aristotle[1] says, "Since Beauty, both in an animal and in everything that is composed of certain parts, ought not only to contain these rules of Proportions, but possess eminently an intrinsic magnitude : for Beauty consists in magnitude and proportions. And since for this reason a very small animal cannot be beautiful, because the observation of it being almost momentary is confused, nor a very large, because the observation is not united ; but the observer's eye attracted from the subordinate parts to the whole : for example, if it were an animal of a thousand furlongs."

Those sculptors who are not guided by the rigid rules of Greek art, copy nature with all her imperfections, nor are they ever able to do justice to

[1] De poetica, vii

the most beautiful parts, much less to select and unite them together ; therefore there is no unity in their works, and often their figures are constrained or in studied modes of position, so that in this respect they do not follow nature, for she is always easy, simple, and graceful. The action should spring from the impulse of the occasion, not studied for effect. Those sculptors who are not of the classical school have no difficulties to contend with, having no fixed principles, for they say that rules cramp their genius. The liberty they enjoy renders them unable to elevate the feelings by their works. Such alone as are guided by the restrictive laws prescribed by Truth and Nature are the most likely of all to produce works which may meet the approval of posterity.

When we pursue this refined art with true ardour, and with the hope of Fame, we feel that we are devoting our lives to a noble object, and when the artistic faculty gives palpable form and substance to our conceptions of the pure and beautiful, the mind is raised above matter, it is then that art receives life and soul by the inspir- ation of genius. When my thoughts dwell in meditation upon some new subject, I then give full scope to my imagination, and by mental energy I begin to see that which I see the embodiment of my conception gradually rising into plastic form within my mind. This is the working of the

inventive faculty. On closing my eyes, the more
vividly do I see the picture which I am about
to form—yes—now I see before me the divine Eros
and Psyche, the celestial Bride and Bridegroom.
They are sitting face to face upon seats of Ivory
and Gold. Psyche negligently attired, with her
delicate form partially exposed, innocent and pure,
enjoying perfect tranquillity and love, her reward
after all her Earthly perturbations. Serenity and
sweetness softens the dignity of her deportment.
She is absorbed in the tenderest contemplation
of her divine protector, whilst at every breath
her transparent wings seem to vibrate with
tremulous motion. Eros with bow and quiver at
his feet, and in his hand silver lyre, sits in repose and
in admiration of his charming Bride. " The first-
born," ever young, bears the stamp of imperishable
beauty. Grace in all his movements, fire and softness in his eyes, wisdom and serene loveliness glow
upon his celestial countenance; his head, crowned
with olives, send forth refulgent light, and rich are
the ambrosial locks which play about his delicate
neck, and splendid are the golden wings which
bear him through the Aether which he breathes.

The heavenly pair are not here alone, for there I
see Hebe with parti-coloured wings and her short
tunic. Zeus has sent his cup-bearer ever fair and
ever young to wait on Love and Psyche in their
golden chamber, and now I see her pouring nectar

into the sculptured cup which she holds in her
delicate hand. This is for Psyche, that she may
drink of the cup of immortality preparatory to her
union with the " first-born," celestial Eros—

> " Source of sweet delight
> Holy and pure, and lovely to the sight."
>   *Orpheus and Eros.*

This my day-dream I have modelled as a basso-
relievo Plato in his " Symposium " says that there
are two Venuses, and two Cupids, one divine and
the other vulgar and Plebeian. Now (Anterota) is
interrupted by Proclus, Divine Love, who abstracts
the soul from the body. Plutarch in " Erotike "
says there were two Loves according to the sentiments of the Egyptians and the Platonists, the
common and the celestial. Alciatus speaking of
Anteros says, " Anteros speaks—' I am not born of
the vulgar or common Venus (Pandemon) I have
nothing to do with vulgar voluptuousness The
vulgar Venus is concerned about base amours, but
I inflame the breast to virtue and to honesty, and
raise the mind to the contemplation of heavenly
things.' "

CHAPTER IX

MR. AND MRS SANDBACH'S VISIT TO ROME—THE HUNTER
AND THE DOG—AURORA—EOS—THE CONDITION OF
SCULPTURE IN ENGLAND

IN the year 1838 came to Rome Mr. Henry
Sandbach of Liverpool and his Lady. She was the
grand-daughter of Roscoe, my early friend. Their
stay being the whole of the winter, gave them
ample opportunities of enjoying Rome, and its
antiquities and its arts; and gave me an opportunity of contemplating the talent and genius of
the descendant of my old friend. Besides that,
she was a poet. I soon perceived her feeling and
taste for my own art in particular. Every one of
my compositions on paper I used to lay before her
as well as those in clay. One subject became the
favourite of Mr. Sandbach as well as of his Lady.
It was a Hunter and his Dog. The idea was
caught from an incident in the street. I observed
a big lad holding a dog by the collar at the moment
of flying at some object, when he let him off.
This caught my eye in a moment. I saw a

204

composition which impressed me. I carried the whole of it in my memory and made my small model in clay. It was ordered by Mr. Sandbach in marble the size of life. This is a statue which I studied with great care and ambition to make it my best work. It is at Mr. Sandbach's house on his estate in North Wales. Besides the Hunter, Mr. Sandbach wished for another statue. He resolved to present to his Lady a work by my hand, the subject of which should be of a kind congenial with her own poetic feeling. This idea suggested by him to me, began to occupy my thoughts deeply, and according to my usual custom I used to retire to the Villa Borghese to be alone in the shade meditating and seeking for ideas, and it was in my solitary wanderings there, that Aurora dawned upon me. I repeated to myself those lines of Milton—

> " Now Morn her rosy steps in the Eastern clime
> Advancing, sowed the earth with orient pearls "

And more and more as I thought of it, did I feel that this would be the very subject for my youthful friend. I wrote the following description of my idea in a letter to her, July, 1842 : " I will give you an idea of the statue, but for the present, only in words It is not a bad thing for an artist to put down in words the spirit of his idea—here it is for you.

" Behold the harbinger of day, Aurora, Goddess of the morning, Mother of the stars and of the winds, just risen from the ocean with the bright star Lucifer glittering over her brow—one foot on the waves, the other softly touching the earth. Aurora, youthful and gay. fresh as the blushing rose, light as the dew, swift as the rising Sun, her Brother. She is clad in a rich and most transparent vest, her delicate limbs are unrestrained and free ; among the numerous folds which collect themselves in playful variety here and there, now waving, now fluttering, now winding about as she glides onward—and onward again through the refreshing breeze.

"Aurora has filled the two vases which she carries in her soft hands with pure dew from the sea, and as she moves onward with swift wings—she casts a serene and dignified glance over the universe and scatters the pearly drops over the earth whereby the flowers are refreshened and expand in the morning sun.

" This subject for a statue is I believe, new, for I have never seen it executed in sculpture. I was encouraged to put it in execution from having seen a fictile vase published by Milengin, upon which is a single figure of Aurora, hovering in the air, looking down upon the earth, and holding in her hands two vases, out of which she is pouring dew upon the earth This is the Greek authority for the two vases in the hands of my statue." The statue was completed in marble, and afterwards it was repeated for Dr. Henry.

THE HUNTER AND THE DOG.

When I was modelling the Hunter and Dog. I had then a very fine model in the prime of his youth, and his proportions correct; besides having this young man, I went often to contemplate the casts from the Elgin marbles at the academy of St. Luke's. The sculptures of the Parthenon, called the Elgin collection, are the most valuable and interesting in existence, we behold works which Phidias himself directed, and the greatest probability is that he designed all the statues and the bassi-relievi, and most likely modelled with his own hands the finest of those works. How highly interesting it is when we feel confident that the great Phidias has had his share in producing what we are dwelling upon, and how he must have conversed daily with his pupils Agoracritus, Alcamenes and Colotes. It may also be supposed that Pericles and Aspasia were occasionally present, led to the artist's studio by the desire of seeing the progress of his works—Yes, the school of Phidias is before our eyes, if we cannot equal those noble examples, we can at least penetrate into their transcendent excellence. Notwithstanding the destruction of Greek art, there are still sufficient works remaining in Europe to enable the moderns to form a grand and pure style of sculpture. At the same time there are great and fatal obstacles in our way; nude statues are not wanted to adorn our buildings nor are they admitted into our

Temples. The public statues which are erected
in our squares and the interior of our mansions do
not require Masters of the Phidian school to produce them   The human figure concealed under
a frock-coat and trousers is not a fit subject for
sculpture, and I would rather avoid contemplating
such objects.

Portrait statues would afford fine study of
drapery, and they might be so executed if there
were an effort made to elevate that part of sculpture
by adopting a monumental costume. The statues
of Generals should be represented with a cloak
covering as much as possible of the offensive dress,
those of distinguished ecclesiastics must be represented as they are in their canonical dress. Those
of statesmen would be ennobled by grand drapery.

When the Government did me the honour of
entrusting to me the execution of the statue of the
late Sir Robert Peel, I was allowed my own way as
to the dress, if they had bound me to the anti-
sculptural costume I was prepared to decline that
work. All being settled to my wish I began to
collect my ideas, and to find out something which
should not be the usual common-place.

It was in the evenings when alone in my room I
put on my Roman cloak, which is very ample, with a
scroll of paper in my hand I acted the orator, going
through various actions again and again. On one of
these occasions, holding the scroll in my right hand,

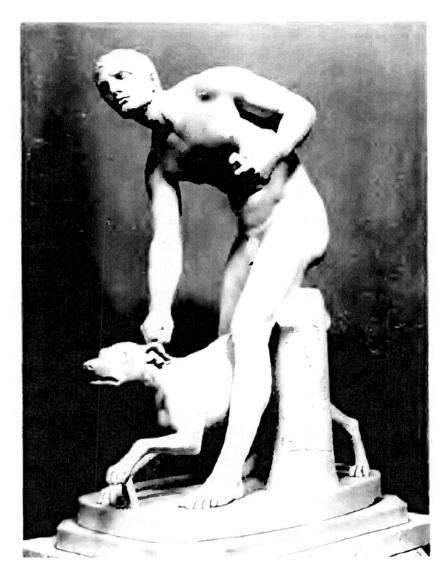

THE HUNTER AND THE DOG

I struck my left hand with it, as if laying down the law. This action, as if having pronounced the last word and waiting the effect upon the audience, is the moment which my statue represents of Sir Robert Peel, now erected in Westminster Abbey I have never seen any portrait statue, ancient or modern, in such a position and expressing the same idea. One of the most classical architects in London stated in a note which I received from him, that "he could not agree with my idea of masquerading John Bull as an ancient Greek."

My reply was that I would not dress him up exactly as an ancient Greek; but that he, the architect, would transgress sadly the rules of good taste and harmony by placing statues in coat and trousers between his Corinthian and Ionic columns, and I added, that to be consistent he should invent a new order of architectural forms to be in unison with such costumes, such statues are to me as obnoxious in a Gothic as they are in a classical building.

The matter-of-fact principles, advocated by many persons—indeed, by all who do not feel pleasure in the contemplation of high art—always produce vulgarity, the literal imitation of matter delights the mass, they are never aware that the image of a great man should always impress the spectator with the character of his intellectual greatness. It should give us an idea of his soul, and this may be done by taste and judgment, without trespassing too much upon the individuality of the person

I know some sculptors who maintain the propriety of representing our great men in the very dress which they wore, but those are men who work more for Gold than Fame; they would never refuse a good job. I can here declare that I have declined such offers. The following remark by Rousseau is applicable to our sublime art : " I have always felt " that the profession of letters was illustrious in " proportion as it was less a trade. It is too difficult " to think nobly when we think for a livelihood." There are scribblers about art who endeavour to denounce the practice of introducing into monuments statues personifying the moral virtues of the deceased ; so they would reduce monumental sculpture to simply the statue of the person, and that must be in frock-coat and cravat. I have read in some that " The practice of personifying natural and moral qualities seems to have been coeval with Grecian poetry and religion ; it was not, however, by any means peculiar to Greece, and will probably be found wherever poetry exists."

The prospect of advancing high sculpture in England seems to me to be far distant. Were I to meet a young sculptor of strong genius and ardent ambition I could tell him from my experience what would be necessary to enable him to become great in the high department of his art.

It is a Roman education for ten years under the tuition of a great master. At the age of thirty he ought to be prepared by his acquired knowledge and experience to begin with confidence a work that would transmit his name to posterity. I do not believe it possible to become great without such advantages. Sculpture is a most difficult and fastidious art which must combine refinement of taste, beauty of form, and purity of style. The greatest sculptors of this age have studied at Rome. The Governments of all the great nations of Europe, excepting that of England, send pensioned students here, and that is the reason that the style of the public monuments in my own country is generally so feeble.

The following list I sent to the Earl Stanhope at his request

A list of the nations whose Governments send pensioned students to Rome, to study historical painting, sculpture, and architecture.

France   Has an Academy   The number of students is
   Five painters   Two landscape painters   Two medal engravers
   Five sculptors   Two engravers   Two musicians
   Five architects
   Each student is pensioned for five years   The French Academy costs the Government in money one hundred and five thousand francs per annum
Austria   Sends pensioned students
Prussia
Saxony
Tuscany
Naples   Has an Academy

Russia   Students have £160 each per annum and £40 for the journey
          to Rome and £40 for his return   Each is pensioned for
          six years

Spain
Mexico
Denmark
Sweden
Belgium
Carrara

" ROME.

" MY LORD,

" In the year 1844 I visited England after an absence of twenty-seven years. The late Sir Robert Peel sent for me. I waited upon him, and he said that the Government had some idea of sending students to Rome, and he wished me to give him what information I could upon such a subject from my long experience of the practice of Foreign Nations. With reference to his question as to the propriety of sending English students to Rome, I was entirely ignorant of the state of sculpture in England, but since my arrival I had been examining the public monuments, and that I could see the defects of style and feebleness which prevailed in the best of them; likewise the absence of the grand principles and severe simplicity with that perfect execution imbibed at Rome. The English Government spend large sums to erect public monuments but contribute nothing towards the training of their students. I had seen some who had natural powers, but wanted the advantages given to young sculptors of the continent, that is a

Roman education for six years. I have visited England a few times since, and the above are still my sentiments. Every young sculptor in England bungles his way as he can; nor do they visit, generally speaking, each other's studios, which at Rome is the universal practice, and more, they point out each other's errors while their models are still in clay.

" If the English Government were to follow the example of other nations they would in the course of time have public monuments that would do more honour to the nation. My object in making these remarks is my anxious desire to see sculpture in England upon an equality with the productions of other nations.

" To the Earl Stanhope.
" *24th March*, 1857."

CHAPTER X

THERE appeared in Rome a boy of twelve years old
of most extraordinary beauty of face and figure,
and whilst painters and sculptors were copying him
I felt very desirous to avail myself of a model
so unusually beautiful. I conceived the design of
a statue of Cupid naked. I represented Eros
caressing a butterfly upon his breast, while with
his right hand he is drawing an arrow to pierce it.
I called it 'Love tormenting the soul.' I spent
three months upon the clay model, working at it
almost constantly. I afterwards executed it in
marble for the late Lord Saye and Sele, repeated it
afterwards for Mr. R. V. Yates of Liverpool, and
also for Mr. Holford. I look upon this statue as
one of my best works.

My next was a statue of Proserpine stooping to
gather flowers in the fields of Enna, she kneels on
one knee, and turns her head in surprise and alarm
at the approach of Pluto. While in the act of

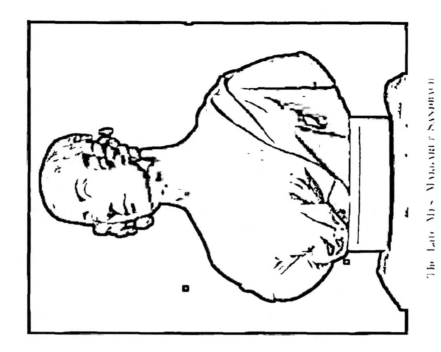

The Late Mrs. Margaret Sandwich

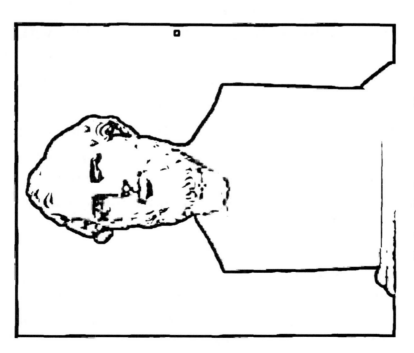

The Late H. B. Simpson Esq

plucking flowers, she is about to spring up from her knee to fly. During the modelling of this statue a young English gentleman caused me much annoyance by running away with a beautiful model I had engaged and carrying her off to England before my work was finished. This statue I executed in marble for Mr Abblett of Llanbedr Hall in North Wales, and repeated it for Dwar-kanath Tagore in Calcutta, and according to his own account it excited great attention there.

In consequence of the following circumstance the second portrait statue of Huskisson was designed. It was proposed by a gentleman in Liverpool that the statue in the cemetery should be removed from its place there to the Custom House. It was found to be much against the feelings of Mrs. Huskisson to remove it, but she requested to be allowed to present a statue to be placed in the Custom House. This offer was accepted, and I was employed by Mrs. Huskisson to model a new statue eight feet high of her late husband.

Although the first statue met with the approbation of the best judges in Rome, I set to work with a determination to surpass it; and it has been generally acknowledged that I have succeeded. The first statue was represented in the act of un-rolling a scroll as if about to utter the first sentence of his speech. The second is represented in a moment of deep thought, with the left hand raised

before the chest, a slight action in the fingers as if
calculating, and the right hand hangs down holding
a scroll.   Both statues are bare-necked, covered with
a mantle falling in large and magnificent folds : a
mode of attiring the statues of our great men
contrary to the ideas of our committees, but not so
to those of true taste.

During the modelling of this statue Mrs. Huskisson returned to Rome, witnessed the progress
of it, and caused many improvements in the
countenance, which made this one a better likeness
than the former.   She herself also considered this
statue the superior one.   These circumstances
brought me to the notice and society of Mrs.
Huskisson, in whom I found a most talented, warm,
and generous friend.   She sympathised most
earnestly in my fame ; and she was the principal
cause of my rousing myself from my twenty-seven
years' stay in Rome and coming to England to place
the statue in the summer of 1844.   I proceeded
to Liverpool for this purpose and found on
examination that the place destined for it in the
long room of the Custom House was quite
unsuitable, and the only place in the building where
there was a proper light could not be obtained.
Mrs. Huskisson, therefore, decided to cast the said
statue in bronze : which was done in Munich by
Muller, and it stands now in the area in front of
the Custom House in the open air.   It was placed

there on the 15th of October 1847, during my second visit to Liverpool, when I was present with my friends Mr. and Mrs Lawrence, the late Sir Robert Peel, Lord Sandon, and others. On my first visit to Liverpool Mr. Lawrence with his friends and the principal gentlemen there honoured me with a public dinner at the Exchange rooms.

I had been applied to by a committee at Glasgow to execute a statue of the late Mr. Kirkman Finlay to be placed in the Merchants' Hall in that town. When the statue arrived there during my stay in England in 1844 I visited Scotland for the first time and witnessed the placing of the statue, which met with the approbation of the sons of Mr. Finlay and of his friends. The principal gentlemen of Glasgow did me the honour to invite me to a public dinner, when Mr Alison was in the chair, and I was much gratified by the kindness which he and the other gentlemen showed me on that occasion When I visited the City I was surprised to see so many public monuments erected, and all by the best sculptors. I thought the statue of General Moore, by Flaxman, one of his best; as well as that of Watt by Chantrey. I examined the Equestrian Statue of the Duke of Wellington by Marochetti, and the horse is very clever. I left Glasgow with grateful recollections of its very kind and good people I stayed at the house of my hospitable friends Mr and Mrs. Graham Gilbert,

and during my stay he painted my portrait, and
since I find he presented it to the Academy there.

In the year 1842 the present Emperor of Russia,[1]
then Hereditary Grand Duke, came to Rome.
One day, three or four Russian gentlemen with
Mr. Lounitz, a Russian sculptor of talent, called and
informed me of the intention of His Imperial
Highness to visit my studio the following day at
one o'clock, saying, that if he did not arrive at a
quarter after one I was not to wait, for in that case
another appointment would be fixed.

The Grand Duke was in my studio ten minutes
after one, he was accompanied by several persons,
and my friend Lounitz the sculptor ; he spoke
English well, and was very agreeable, examining
everything with great interest. In the course of a
few days two of his retinue and Mr. Lounitz
returned and informed me that H.I.H. had fixed
upon two of my works, and wished them to be
executed in marble for him, and that the price of
each work must be fixed : this was written down.
The works were, my group of Psyche carried by
Zephyrs and the Cupid disguised as a shepherd.
This commission was finished in three years, and
my performances have their place in the Imperial
Palace at St Petersburg.

Nearly opposite my door I had a rival, and
H.I.H. went over to him and ordered a statue of

---

[1] That is Nicholas I., 1796-1855

a nymph; this rival was Richard Wyatt, who had
been studying in Rome for many years, and with
indefatigable labour; he as well as myself had been
scholars of Canova, but not for any length of time,
for that great sculptor died in the year 1822; then
both of us had recourse to Thorwaldsen for instruction. Wyatt had acquired the purest style, and
his statues were finished to the utmost of his
power; his *forte* was female figures, and he was
clever in composition and the harmony of lines;
drapery was also a great study with him. His statues
are remarkably chaste in sentiment, refined in
character, and graceful in action: he had a strong
feeling for the beautiful.

Wyatt's practice was universally as follows:
whenever he made a clay sketch for a new subject
he would shut it up out of sight for six or more
months, then bring it out for trial; if he continued
to like it he would then begin his clay model life-
size, availing himself of as many living models as he
could find, and he always cast the joints when
those parts were beautiful in nature—indeed the
Roman sculptors make a great study of the joints,
hands, and feet

There was a compact between Wyatt and myself,
which was, to point out each other's defects un-
reservedly; and I felt that each of us benefited by
the judgment of the other. Besides the general
feeling of rivalry which existed between Wyatt and

myself where art was concerned, there was one
point of contact in which I must confess he was
generally my superior, namely, in his habit of early
rising, for though I always arrived at the Caffé
Greco to breakfast before sunrise. I constantly
found him already established there, sitting with a
wax taper in his hand, and reading the daily papers
over his coffee So soon as the daylight dawned
we proceeded to take our walk as usual on the
Monte Pincio; after half an hour's exercise we
descended the Hill to our studios in the Via
Fontanella-Babuino.

CHAPTER XI

THE REVOLUTION OF 1848—GARIBALDI

IN the year 1848 a state of political commotion was excited in Rome by a combination of various circumstances, and in the following year Count Rossi, the Papal minister, was assassinated on the steps of the Cancelleria, and the Pope felt it necessary to take flight to the Neapolitan territories. Such a state of things could not but have its effects among the artists at Rome. The Muses are said to be silent amidst the clash of arms

Although I must say that I personally experienced no molestation during this difficult period in the prosecution of my own works, and was certainly surprised at the forbearance and good conduct of the Roman people in general, in spite of the incitements to mischief of certain demagogues, yet I am perfectly aware that the same might not apply to native artists, and that they found it necessary, for various reasons, to absent themselves for a time from their usual avocations. I believe this to have been the case with Cavaliere Tenerani

I

He held an official employment under the Papal
Government, and he was moreover the compatriot
and friend of Count Rossi.   It is no small praise to
him, and affords no trifling proof of his devotion to
art, that in spite of all this interruption to his usual
occupation he has since returned apparently with
fresh ardour to his former studies, and has produced
works from his chisel which are entirely worthy of
his earlier efforts.   I have stated lately that during
the tumults in Rome the populace conducted themselves with more order than is usual in such cases.
I cannot therefore be supposed to be desirous
of alluding to acts of assassination and private
plunder with which the story of this time is too
much tarnished : but as these are now matters
of history, and as they have been reported and
commented upon by all the journals of Europe, I
shall not be doing my duty as an actual observer
on the spot at the time, if I did not relate what I
actually witnessed.

One day when I was working at one of my
statues, two English friends entered and said,
" Have you heard the news ? " I said that my
man tells me that Count Rossi has been assassinated, but I do not believe it.   They said to me,
" Pray, put on your coat and come out with us. '
I did so, and arrived with them at the Corso,
where we found every house on each side with flags
and tapestry, purple and gold displayed in token

of rejoicing at the horrid event which had just taken place.

In the evening of that day insulting songs were sung under the window of the widow,[1] who was conveyed in a private carriage of the Pope's that night to Civita Vecchia. I have understood that the town was universally illuminated in celebration of her husband's murder.

After the Pope had fled from Rome, the storm gradually increased, and still some English people lingered there. among them were Lord and Lady M. with their children. Her Ladyship was very handsome and peculiarly fascinating. One day I was dining with them, and when their English physician came into the room, her Ladyship said, "Well, Doctor, what news? How are they getting on?" "Badly," said he, and then related as he was coming from St. Peter's. and just as he had crossed the Bridge of St. Angelo, he saw a crowd of people advancing, and in front of the mob they had two prisoners—common-looking men, one with his head bound round with a bloody white handkerchief. By this time the Doctor was close upon them, when a man with a musket and bayonet ran one of the prisoners through from the back, the bayonet entering between the pelvis bone and the last rib; the victim fell upon his face, when numbers kept stabbing him as well as the other

---

[1] Madame Sontag, the celebrated singer

man, both on the ground. There was a pool of
blood, and the Doctor said that some men, and two
or three women, collected the blood in their hands
and then washed their faces with it, clapping
their bloody hands aloft in air, and crying out,
"Throw them into the Tiber!" The Doctor had
already inquired what they had done, and was
told they were Jesuits in disguise. The bodies
were then dragged by the heels upon the Bridge of
St. Angelo and then thrown over into the Tiber.
So there was an end of them. Afterwards, it was
proved that the men were poor working-people
and slaughtered under a mistake. All of us
listened with great attention to the Doctor's statement. Her Ladyship looked all the time un-
comfortable, and her sister particularly so The
servant entered, and announced dinner. At dinner,
the company were pretty cheerful, and her Ladyship brightened up. Next to me sat an English
gentleman who had been in Mexico when Garibaldi
was there. He said, " Garibaldi is a very brave
fellow—he is an amphibious animal, it's all the
same to him to fight on the water or on land.
At Mexico he commanded a legion, a motley
corps assembled from all parts of the world, but
when in action," added he, " they obeyed commands
beautifully, moved as regularly as clock-work and
fought with great valour."

At this period Garibaldi was in the Roman

Provinces maintaining himself and troops by levying contributions. At one town they closed the gates of the city against him, but he soon sent a message to say that if they did not open the gates he would do so for them with his artillery. The Pope before his flight sent a General to attack him. but Garibaldi was not to be frightened.

I bade good-night to my Lord and family and walked home alone. the streets at eleven o'clock at night were very lonely, and I met only now and then a solitary individual and no one would allow me to come too close to them, but kept to one side as I did myself. keeping at large and having small pistols loaded All this precaution arose from the fear of being stabbed. Every evening the mass of the people were indoors at dusk.

The time arrived when the English who had tarried so long at Rome were anxious to quit, but they found it was too late, they could not get away, and the frequency of assassination began to alarm them, not that they were in any danger themselves. The reason that they could not leave the town was, the authorities would not give permission for horses. which afterwards was obtained, and they all left Rome.

Rome was fast filling with grim-looking fellows armed in various ways. with long wild black hair. and unclean long beards. The quiet people of

Rome wondered where they all came from : we saw the entrance of Garibaldi at the head of two legions; the Lancers were most respectably mounted and the Lombardi infantry were fine-looking soldiers, with their round hats and cock's feathers Garibaldi was under the middle size, well-made, and very handsome features, and a fine long beard : his dress was beautiful, a red tunic, and his waistband, which was black, was well-fitted with small arms and a fine sabre.   His manner was frank, natural and manly ; he was much esteemed by his companions in arms, and everybody spoke of his bravery and that he did not plunder to enrich himself

One day a French priest was stabbed in the streets, he was stretched on the pavement, and some people stood round him looking at him dying, when a native working sculptor, called in England carver, entered the ring, and looking upon the bleeding priest, with a heavy stick in his hand he gave him a blow upon the skull with all his force to put him out of his pain.   The poor priest breathed no more.

After the French army was settled here the General ordered a commission to examine into the affair of the French priest , our sculptor was arrested, tried, and condemned to death, but the French Government commuted his punishment to hard labour for life ; he was sent to Toulon.

He could not bear his new situation and the labour, which was not sculpture, for he had talent and earned money. He died in less than a year. He once attempted to kill one of my men, a native of Carrara.

Among the English who were in Rome at that time was Mrs. E., a pretty little widow, with her young daughter, who was much excited and felt great interest in the cause of the party who called themselves the liberals. This lady moved in a high class of society, and she had become acquainted with Garibaldi and felt the greatest interest in him and his affairs. One day I went to the Piazza del Popolo to see the departure of Garibaldi with half a regiment of the 'Lombardi', for some days detachments had been sent from Rome to give battle to the King of Naples who was encamped at Albano. Garibaldi was following to join the whole force sent there. Garibaldi went to take his leave of Mrs. E., and it was from her house he came to join his men. It was reported that he said to her on rising, " Is your daughter too old to be kissed ? " and her reply was, " Oh, General ! No lady is too old to be kissed. '

I will mention an incident which occurred to me soon after Pio Nono gave his general amnesty. At that period I used to dine at a Trattoria in the Piazza di Spagna; one day there I sat down to table by the side of my friend Penry Williams, the

well-known painter : I said, "Observe that little
man, how his eyes are fixed upon me." He was
short, with rich black hair and beard, his eyes bright.
He came right up to me—"Signor Gibson," said
he, "you do not seem to know me." "Who are
you?" said I. "Have I not waited upon you at
this table three years ago?" "Bentornato!
where have you been all this time?" said I.
"In the Galleys," said he. "What for?" "Signor
Gipison, I am a patriot." I bowed to him, and
said, "Oh, I understand you, I suppose you are
indebted to Pio Nono for the liberty which you
are now enjoying." "Yes, I am," he replied. "I
advise you not to lose your liberty again." I then
inquired of my friend where he had been imprisoned so long. "At Civita Castellana," he said.
"I was condemned for seven years." The Castle
was crowded with political prisoners, the poor ones
were upon short allowance, the sons of the rich
were supplied with money, and permitted to
purchase what they liked to make them more
comfortable. He was fortunate, he added, that
he had learnt a little cooking by observations
in the kitchen, and the gentlemen prisoners elected
him their cook, so he was well off as to feeding,
and he said, with a peculiar air of importance and
affected modesty, "Signor Gipison, I am a poet."
I bowed instantly again ; he said, "Yes, I was
elected Cook and Poet to the Patriots at Civita

Castellana." " In what class of poetry did you exercise your talents?" " I employed my humble abilities in writing epigrams." " What were the subjects you wrote upon?" " Liberty, Equality, and I touched up the Church and priests, and all religions as the inventions of the ecclesiastical order. My poetry amused my fellow prisoners, but they did not all agree with my opinions upon religion. My skill as a cook gave universal satisfaction " I said to him, " With respect to the art of cooking, Atheneus relates that there was a cook in Greece acquired great renown because he could roast one half of a pig whilst the other was boiling." " Ah, Signor Gipison, those ancient Greeks were great liars, but they could fight for Liberty."

My little friend, waiter, cook, patriot, and poet, must be left to follow his humble but diversified labours for some time to come, but he is destined to flourish once more, for Fate, more powerful than Love, has doomed him to the galleys again, and it will be seen that by good fortune he was snatched from the hands of Justice and set free once more. I have always admired the exclamation of Madame Roland when she appeared on the scaffold, looking up at the statue of Justice, she said, " Oh, what crimes are committed in thy name!"

When the Pope would grant no more concessions to his subjects, their glorifications of him gradually subsided. and now and then a priest fell by the sly hand of the assassin.

My friend Wyatt used at that time to dine at a Trattoria in the Via Condotti, and one day he told me that he had made a new acquaintance, an Irish priest who had lately come to Rome, that he was a very gentleman-like man, very agreeable and amiable. One evening, at dusk, Wyatt and the priest came out of the Trattoria together, bade each other good-night, Wyatt turned to the Piazza di Spagna, whilst the priest walked down the Via Condotti ; when he had proceeded some way (as afterwards related to Wyatt), a little man with bright black eyes, curly hair, and a long beard, suddenly struck at his throat with a knife, but the priest, equally quick, saved his throat, and the knife struck him in the palm of his hand. The assassin fiercely repeated the blow, and again the priest received another wound in the palms of his hands Two young men, National Guards, who saw the act at a little distance, ran up with their drawn swords, and the first one in advance cried out to the assassin, " If you stir, I will run you through." The man then gave himself up. The priest was bleeding much from his wounds, and leaning against the wall of a shop, a woman came out: seeing the poor priest pitied by some of the persons round him, she asked them to help him into her shop. which they did. The priest was

JOHN GIBSON

(after a portrait-sketch by Penry Williams in 1839).

quite a stranger in Rome. The woman gave him a chair, and soon she bound up his bleeding hands with linen, and some of the persons present proposed to get a coach, and they offered to accompany him to the hospital in the Corso, where his wounds were dressed, and then he was taken to his home. One of the young surgeons attended him. An account of the affair was registered while the assassin was in prison.

One day the priest was summoned to attend at the prison; he went there, and he was shortly conducted to a large room, and before him stood a row of prisoners, and he was told, if he saw among them the man who had stabbed him, to go up and put his finger upon him. The priest instantly went up, and touched a man who turned out to be no other than my little friend the waiter, cook, patriot, poet and assassin. He was tried and condemned to fifteen years in the Galleys. This happened previous to the Pope's departure from Rome.

In the course of a few months after this affair, whilst I was dining at the Trattoria, I asked the waiter what caused the rejoicing which I heard throughout the house. He said, with great excitement, that the Government of the Triumviri had liberated my friend from the Galleys, "but," said I, "he was condemned under the Pope's Government to fifteen years' imprisonment for wounding the Irish priest." The fellow then said, "As he had only stabbed a priest, they have liberated him." Soon after, my little, active waiter called upon an English painter, my friend, and he said to him that he had intentions of going to London, that he had plenty of gold, and he asked what might be the expense of his journey to England

Two years after, I enquired from a companion of the person I have described what had become of him, and he whom I addressed said that he had heard that the little fellow, who had played so many parts, had been fortunate at last, for he had been informed that he had become married to a "Signora Inglese" in London This latter piece of information I confess I considered to be untrue.

I heard after that this rogue confessed that he thought the priest whom he stabbed was an Italian, that he did not know that he was an Irishman.

Sometime after I saw a procession going down the Corso, it was a young man on an ass, upon his breast was a label, on which you read that he was guilty of carrying the prohibited knife. He was accompanied by a guard of soldiers on each side of him, and by many people. He was started from the Piazza del Popolo to the end of the Corso, and at the Piazza Venezia there was a stage made on which he was to stand for a short time to be looked at When he ascended the steps and got on the stage, he turned round, facing the people, raised his right hand aloft with the thumb and two first fingers up, the third and little fingers bent down, and with an air of benign majesty he gave the people the benediction in imitation of the Holy Father. For this act of impiety he was afterwards retained in prison for some weeks.

The prohibited knife is a real dagger which shuts up like a clasp knife, but it is made on purpose for assassination. When the disturbance had made considerable advancement, those very prohibited knives were sold and carried about publicly in the streets of Rome Of this fact I had a proof at the time, in the following manner. One evening I was sitting in the Caffé, in the Piazza di Spagna, and in came a man whom I knew; he kept a shop of objects of fine arts, and he was for years afflicted with occasional fits of madness. Whenever the fits came on, notice used to be sent to the authorities, a coach was brought to his door, and he was taken to the madhouse, there kept till he recovered, then set at liberty to attend to his business.

During our Republic the madman was not taken sufficient care of. At this time, unluckily, his fit came upon him, and he had been raving up and down for three or four days. It was evening when he came into the Caffé and recognised me,

seating himself upon a stool opposite to where I
was placed ; he began muttering to himself very
wildly ; we were sitting on divans which went
round the little room.   I could see into the next
room, and I beheld a pedlar who had just entered.
and he put his basket upon the marble table ; the
madman, turning round his head, also saw the
pedlar.   He got up and went to him and looked
into the basket, when I saw him taking out the
horrid instrument of vengeance, the prohibited
knife.   It glistened in the sunlight.   He grasped the
dagger, fixing his eyes upon me.   He was advancing.   I, as quick as thought, turned my eyes to
the right and to the left to fly, but he was up and
stood before me ; I sat still and felt no fear.   I
looked at him calmly when he drew back the
dagger and struck out with the weapon violently
within an inch of my body, and then, retiring it,
said. " Signor Professore, I will give you this, take
it."   I was afraid to raise my hand to receive the
dagger for fear he should change his mind and stab
me.   The madman then left me and returned the
instrument into the basket.

The attack of the madman upon me was so sudden
that no one dared to move ; there was no chair
in the room with which I could defend myself.   I
said to my friends that my life hung upon a thread,
and Doctor Albetis, who sat near, observed that it
was a most critical moment, although I did not

feel the least fear at the instant, yet after the affair was over and the man gone, I felt cold, and a slight tremor came on for a short time. The madman was taken by the authorities next morning to the mad-house. I have now given a proof that those instruments were carried about the streets, and sold, at the time, in Rome.

During the troubles Don Carlo Torlonia died; he was always the favourite of the Romans. I saw his funeral, which was very splendid; as he was Colonel of a regiment of the National Guards, the military display on that occasion was very fine. They glittered magnificently by torch-light, infantry and cavalry, and there was a long procession of indigent ladies with wax torches in their hands, whom the deceased had assisted by his private charity, also one of the young girls whom he supported and educated. A great concourse of the people followed. The last time I saw Don Carlo Torlonia he looked ill, and he asked me if I had heard from Mrs. Huskisson; he added in a low tone, "Cara Signora"; these were the last words which I ever heard him utter.

My object is not to dwell upon the Roman revolution, their Republic lasted but a short time: when it was proclaimed to the people all Rome was taken by surprise: it came upon them quite unexpectedly. The Catholic Powers soon desired to replace the Pope, a formidable French army entered Rome, and soon all was quiet again. I saw the entrance of the Pope into Rome. There was a great display of French troops on that day. Pio Nono looked well and happy, all Rome was up, and he was received with shouts everywhere, as he moved along the streets.

As time advanced some of the French soldiers were stabbed, that is, when a single soldier walked alone in any out-of-the-way place. One morning I read a proclamation on the walls, from which I gathered that the French General made known to the Romans that having tried what mild measures would do, and they having failed in producing their proper effect, he now had decided to adopt a more vigorous course The Proclamation ran thus : " Be it known to all the people of Rome that any person found with any cutting or stabbing instrument upon his person, or knife of any sort, shall be shot."

In the course of two or three days after the proclamation had been all over the City, a man stabbed a soldier, was caught, tried and condemned, and almost directly after another was discovered with a stabbing knife upon him, and at his trial he was asked what his object was in carrying the prohibited instrument? His reply was, " I procured that knife to stab a Frenchman." He was condemned, and they were both shot together. I saw them near to my studio in the Piazza del

Popolo. They descended from the car perfectly calm, and walked with a firm step to the spot hard by, where they knelt down. The instant we heard the report of the muskets they fell motionless.

From that day to the present no French soldier has received the slightest insult as far as I know. The conduct of these troops in Rome has been most excellent, remarkably quiet and inoffensive, and when spoken to they are very polite. During all the disturbances here not one of the natives ever broke a lamp or a pane of glass, nor were any one of the foreigners residing at Rome molested in the slightest degree.

CHAPTER XII

THE REVOLUTION OF 1849—THE BOMBARDMENT OF ROME—DEATH OF WYATT

April,
1849.
IN the year 1849 we were much disturbed by the public commotions at Rome. I cannot say that the Italians molested any of us, but it was most disagreeable to be in a place in such a state of uproar. When the French army arrived at Civita Vecchia, I advised my friend Wyatt to join me in leaving Rome, but he said, "There is no doubt that the French will have to bombard this town, I will stay and see it all—yes, it will be a sight well worth seeing in one's life."

When the French army was four miles from our walls, I ran away and left my companion to his fate, as well as all my statues to take their chance. During my flight to Florence, the French were preparing to bombard Rome, and the Austrians were occupied in cannonading Bologna, Ancona, and Leghorn.

I was at the Baths of Lucca when I received a letter from Wyatt, parts of which I extracted in a letter to Miss Skerrett on business, to be laid before the Queen.

"To Miss Skerrett.

"Dear Madam,

"Will you kindly lay the following before Her Majesty the Queen, with my humble duty? The statue of Her Majesty I have finished according to my promise and the polisher would have completed his part of the work had he not been disturbed by some communications threatening assassination, as he was considered a ' Nero,' as the Pope's party is called, the more so as his son is a priest. I advised him thereupon to leave Rome for Porta d'Anzio. He took my advice, and in consequence of his absence H.M. cannot have the statue so soon as it was promised."

I have inserted parts from the letter which I had received from Wyatt, where he related that he saw the preparations which the French were making to attack the city on the side of the Piazza del Popolo. Anticipating a bombardment so close to our studios, he reported that he had crossed over to my studio with a few men and moved my statue of the Queen to a corner of the room where it stood, and made a roof over it with strong boards, so that if shells or cannon balls fell through the roof upon it, they might roll

e, off. In the course of three days after, the attack
began about three o'clock in the morning.   Wyatt
was startled out of his sleep by the thunder of
artillery, the hissing of the shells, and the smashing
of the tiles of the houses all round about: he
jumped out of bed, which was placed immediately
under the roof, dressed, and came down the winding
staircase to his working rooms, which were on the
ground floor where his works stood   After he had
been a little while there, the voice of war was
louder and louder, when, in an instant, a grenade
came through the window into the room where he
stood, burst, and one of the pieces grazed his
shoulder and another bit knocked the light out of
his hand ; his arm was benumbed, and he was left
in the dark in the midst of smoke and dust from
the broken side wall of the window ; he added,
" I had a very narrow escape."   It appeared from
his letter that a shell had fallen close to the door
of my own studio, when the women opposite, seeing
fire and smoke, cried out, " The Englishman's
studio is on fire," but the shell did no harm.   In
our neighbourhood lived a Scotch tradesman who
had a wife and two little children ; they were all
sleeping in the same room in the upper part of the
house, the noise frightened them and they started
up and fled below, most fortunately, for very soon
after a shell fell through the roof and burnt in their
bedroom.

The movement of the French towards this side of the town was merely a feint in order to conceal their real point of attack which was in fact on Monte Jamcolo where they actually entered near the Porta San Pancrazio. All the above I copied in my letter to Miss Skerrett which I put in the post at the Baths of Lucca. In return, I received a letter from her by the next post which informed me that she had laid my letter before the Queen, and that her Majesty said that it was a very interesting epistle, and she added, " Poor Mr. Wyatt, I am so sorry for poor Wyatt, he shall make me a statue. Write to Mr. Gibson directly and desire him to inform Mr. Wyatt of my wish— yes, he shall make two statues for me, some graceful subjects—say that he must send me sketches soon in a letter "

I accordingly wrote from the Baths of Lucca to Rome and informed my friend of all that H.M. had expressed respecting himself. Wyatt lived to finish one statue only, and the other was completed under my superintendence. The Queen has four statues by Wyatt and they are at Osborne. The statue of a Nymph which he made for the Hereditary Grand Duke of Russia was so much admired by his mother that she had it placed in her own sitting-room, this was told me by a Russian gentleman who saw it there.

The statue of a young Huntress taking a thorn

out of her dog's foot which he made for the King
of Naples, he repeated for our Queen.

No sculptor in England has produced female
statues to be compared to those of Wyatt, and the
judges at the great exhibition in London of 1851
very justly awarded him one of the four first-class
gold medals. This honour was conferred upon
him after his death, for he died in the year 1850.
His superiority in style, refinement, and truth to
nature was owing to a long training which he had
gone through at Rome, where he was surrounded
by so many powerful rivals sufficient to excite his
emulation and where their works were constantly
open to his inspection

Wyatt died of a short illness, when I was on a
visit to England. It was a neglected cold which
attacked the throat, when in one night the inflam-
mation increased so rapidly that he was suffocated ;
as nobody lived in that part of the building, he
had no one near to call the doctor, nor to assist
him. He was found in the morning on the floor,
speechless and gasping his last, with his head, arms
and legs bruised and bleeding, having knocked
himself about in his agony. It was Mr. Spence, a
young sculptor of great merit, who was the first to
run there in the morning, and saw him breathe his
last. Mr. Spence finished some of his works which
were left behind him

Wyatt was remarkably modest, retiring, and

very shy, an excellent judge of Art, and he had a contempt for those mediocrity artists who push on, and puff themselves up, particularly that system in London of newspaper eulogiums on mediocrity.

When I was modelling a second bust of her Majesty at Osborne in 1850, one day the Queen, in presence of Prince Albert, said, " I expected long ago to have seen Mr. Wyatt's name on the list of Academicians." "So did I," said H.R.H I then related that Sir C. Eastlake had proposed Wyatt at the Academy, and that there was a considerable party in favour of electing him, but that Sir Francis Chantrey was opposed to it, and by his influence he gained a majority against Sir C Eastlake's proposition. The Queen darted her eyes upon me and said, " Sir Francis Chantrey was a good man." " He was," said I, " but he had, with many other home-bred artists, a strong prejudice against Rome, which showed that he took a narrow view of Art;" but I believe that Sir F Chantrey said on that occasion, in defence of his exclusion of Mr Wyatt, that the existing law of the Academy, which prescribed that the candidate should be a resident in England, must be adhered to strictly. In my case it would appear that this rule had either been neglected or waived, owing to Sir C. Eastlake's intervention.

The Academy had been informed of the observation which H.M. had made to me respecting

Mr. Wyatt, and they decided to elect him at the first
opportunity—but too late. I repeated the above
conversation to Mr. Wyon, who was then engaged
in modelling a medallion of H.M., and I recommended him to make it known at the next
meeting of the Academy, which he afterwards did;
and they accordingly decided that he should be
elected at the next opening. Unhappily, before
this could take place, Mr. Wyatt was no more.

Mr. Wyatt's relations were going to erect a
small monument over their brother's grave at
Rome, but I requested, as a friend, to be allowed
to perform that duty. I have done so, and sculptured his handsome profile with the following
inscription :—

TO THE MEMORY
OF RICHARD WYATT SCULPTOR
BORN IN LONDON ON THE 3 OF MAY 1785
DIED IN ROME ON THE 28 OF MAY 1850
HE PRACTISED HIS ART IN ROME
29 YEARS.

HIS WORKS WERE UNIVERSALLY ADMIRED
FOR THEIR PURITY OF TASTE GRACE
AND TRUTH OF NATURE

THE PRODUCTIONS OF HIS GENIUS ADORN
THE ROYAL PALACES OF ENGLAND
ST PETERSBURG AND NAPLES
AS WELL AS THE RESIDENCES OF THE NOBILITY
AND GENTRY OF HIS OWN COUNTRY
HE WAS REMARKABLE FOR HIS MODESTY HIS
HIGH SENSE OF HONOUR AND BENEVOLENCE
ERECTED BY JOHN GIBSON R A SCULPTOR
AS A TOKEN OF AFFECTION AND ADMIRATION

CHAPTER XIII

VISIT TO ENGLAND—SIR ROBERT PEEL'S STATUE—RAIL-
WAY ADVENTURES—THE BANE OF COMPETITIONS

I RETURNED to Rome in the year 1850. My
statue of the Queen being finished, I introduced
coloured ornaments upon the mantle, diadem, &c.
I was pleased with the effect, but it was condemned by all the English who came to Rome;
not one had I on my side, but all the artists,
Germans and natives, tacitly approved; all the
well-informed were aware that it was a practice
almost universally adopted among the Greeks.
I wrote to Miss Skerrett to inform H.M. that
I had adorned the statue a little with colours in
spite of the objections raised to it by all of our
countrymen then at Rome. I requested that in
case H.M. should not approve of the effect of
the colours which I had applied, that she would
allow them to remain at least a twelvemonth,
inasmuch as H.M. would be able more justly to
appreciate the real value of the effect of the
colours by frequent examination of the work
which I had sent.

The statue arrived in England, and agreeable to
my request it was allowed to go to the Exhibition
of the Royal Academy ; it was a fine bone to pick
for the scribblers on art.   I had arrived in London,
and was again lodged with Mrs. Huskisson, when
one day we read a rich article upon the Queen's
statue which began upon the innovation of introducing colours, which they condemned with angry
contempt, and they added that the statue itself
" was a total failure, and bore no resemblance to
the Queen "   In the meanwhile it was generally
admired by the public. for they crowded daily to
the sculpture room to see it.

One day I received commands to attend at
Buckingham Palace ; I went, and after waiting
for a short time in a small sitting-room. H.R.H.
Prince Albert entered ; he was gracious, and giving
me his hand, he said, " Well, I wished to tell you
that the Queen and myself went very early in the
morning, before any one had arrived, to see the
statue, and I am happy to tell you that the Queen
is very much pleased with her statue, and so am I,"
said he, " colours and all," laughing, and he observed
at the same time that he had seen in one of the
daily papers a violent attack upon my work.
" Ignorant scribblers !" said I.   " I have always
a contempt for them, and as to the colours, as
I live, they shall have a stronger dose of Poly-
chrome."

There was a report spread among some people that H.M. was dissatisfied with her statue; however the Queen gave a good proof that this was not the fact, for she ordered me shortly after to make a repetition of the statue for her, and she did not suggest any alteration whatever. The second statue is placed at Osborne It was during that visit to England I received the Government commission for the statue of the late Sir Robert Peel, which when known gave birth to a few articles of great bitterness against Lord John Russell, and depreciating me as a sculptor. The statue of Sir Robert Peel is seven feet high, and I received for that work five thousand guineas. It stands in Westminster Abbey.

I will now mention Earl FitzWilliam's visit to Rome; his Lordship was accompanied by his daughters, Lady Charlotte, Lady Dorothy, and Lady Albreda He visited my studio alone, and after examining all my works he said that he had a wish to decorate his large Hall at Wentworth with two bassi-relievi, and that he had fixed upon the subjects. The moment he said that he had fixed upon the subjects a damp fell upon my mind, for if I did not approve of the subject, I should not have been willing to accept the order. His Lordship named the subjects, saying, that he had great love for horses I then said that I had great admiration for horses, and that I had studied that animal

very much—the anatomy, the action, and its
forms.

It was a subject from the history of England,
knights on horseback in armour. The Gothic
armour was at once unfavourable to sculpture.
I objected to the costume which it would be
necessary to introduce. I tried to impress upon
his mind that the beauty of the human form with
expression was the charm of sculpture. I then
showed him my book of designs. Among my
numerous drawings for bassi-relievi there was one
representing the Hours and the horses of the Sun.
I had that composition on hand for two or three
years, and every now and then improving it; his
Lordship did not say much more at that time, but
he intimated his intention of coming again with
his daughters to see my works.

Earl FitzWilliam revisited my studio with his
ladies, and very soon asked to see my book of
drawings, and particularly wished that I should
point out to him the sketch of the Hours and the
horses of the Sun, which I soon turned to. Lady
Charlotte began to admire it, dwelling upon it,
and then Lady Dorothy and Lady Albreda; in
fact Lady Charlotte advised her father to have it
executed. It was decided upon, and I spent a
long time in modelling that work, and although
I had made many anatomical studies of the horse,
I still made more dissections, and also studied

from the life. His Lordship also ordered the companion to the Hours, it was Phaeton driving the Chariot of the Sun.

I was in England on a visit when my bassi-relievi arrived, and Lord Fitzwilliam invited me to Wentworth to see his architect superintending the placing of my works. I left my kind hostess, Mrs. Huskisson, to go on that journey. She never had faith in my railroad travelling, after I got into a mess on my return from Drayton Manor when I visited the late Sir Robert Peel. I was put down in the wrong town and had to wait for the next train, and to go back to the right station.

It was from the residence of Mr. Cheney, Badger Hall, I proceeded to Wentworth. The train stopped at a small station; seeing a few people getting out, I also descended, when in a moment I saw the train begin to move on On it went, faster and faster, out of sight, with my luggage, and I standing there lost and perplexed. I walked a few paces backward and forward with my head down in disagreeable meditation. Well, thought I, how am I to get to Lord Fitzwilliam? Oppressed with vexation, I thought to myself, "I wish to God that I was on my way back to Rome with a Vetturino," when I observed a policeman fixing his eyes upon me and drawing near slowly, darting his glance through me. I said to the man, "Where is that cursed train gone to? It's off with my luggage, and here I am." He said, " What is the name of the station where you took your ticket ? " " I do not remember, nor do I know the names of any of these places." Then the policeman, cocking his head on one side with a look of contempt, said, " Well, sir, I must confess that you are one of the most stupid persons I have yet met with." A lady with her two pretty young daughters was sitting near, and they stared at me, but I turned away my face, ashamed to be seen by them. I told the policeman that I was going to Wentworth House. He then informed me that my train would go through Birmingham to London and that I must remain where I was till the train would arrive. I did so, and in consequence arrived very late at Wentworth. I told my adventure to Lord Fitz-william and to the ladies: his Lordship immediately despatched one of his servants to telegraph for my things to London ; the answer was " Know nothing of Mr. Gibson's luggage." Then my Lord proposed to lend me some of his clothes to dress for dinner, but as he was taller than myself, I declined his kind offer, and sat at table in my travelling dress.

The next morning I left Wentworth to go after my things, and I was told when I should arrive at Birmingham to ask for the stationmaster. I did so, and told him how I had been left behind, and how my things had been carried off by the train. He began to question me rapidly as to what stations I had come through. "Sir," I said, "I do not know," and put my hand into my pocket and showed him the names written on a piece of paper. His manner was not at all agreeable. Then I thought of the graceful, polite Italians, and my happy Vetturino travelling in my former days. The man with an inquisitive look said, "Sir, may I ask what part of the world you belong to?" "Well, sir, you may," and instantly made up my mind if he should be impertinent and call me stupid, as the other man did, to retaliate.

"I live at Rome, and have been there most of my life, but I am an Englishman, and going back there." "Rome!" the man said with a stare. "Yes, I am a sculptor and work there." He was amazed, and said, "My father was a sculptor, sir, and worked for Flaxman; did you know that great sculptor?" "I did, a little, before I first left England." Upon this information as to my occupation and usual place of residence, this quick, important little fellow's manner became suddenly changed, and he said, "I will have your luggage here this very evening." I then said, "I do not believe that you will succeed so soon as all that." Again he looked over my paper, and said, "Yes, I will telegraph immediately; this very evening your things will be here." I put up at the hotel, and sure enough my things arrived in the evening, and I was thus indebted to this casual discovery that I was a sculptor for the speedy recovery of my luggage.

I had no patience to learn the use of the little railway book, and often Mrs. Huskisson would write out the stations for me whenever I left her on a journey.

I found Earl FitzWilliam and his ladies most delightful people. I modelled a bust of Lady Albreda, and executed it in marble at Rome; it is now at Wentworth House.

I have alluded to the scribblers on art in London, and whilst there I discovered that needy class of men lend themselves to those artists who can afford to encourage them. I have dined a few times with a painter well known to the public, of great merit in his department of art; I was acquainted with this artist at Rome. Every time that I have had the pleasure of dining with him, he had one or two of these scribblers at his table. I was assured that many of the painters and sculptors feast those men of letters. If the men so employed were real judges of art, and honest in their criticisms of the works submitted to them, they might do essential good by producing a correct taste for the arts in their native country.

During my late visits to England, I have had opportunities of acquiring a knowledge of the state of sculpture there, and of those who arrange public monuments. I feel that it is my duty to express my sentiments freely, however presumptuous and ungracious I may be considered by many. If I can direct attention to a most fatal impediment to the advancement of art in our country, I ought to do so boldly.

It is from the experience of forty years' study and practice at Rome, and after having the benefit of intercourse with many of the greatest artists of this age, as well as some enlightened persons who have devoted their time to the contemplation of this subject. I have therefore no hesitation in affirming that nothing but evil consequences must arise to the arts in our country, from the prevailing custom of entrusting the decision upon matters of this kind to a committee composed of a certain number of members collected from different classes of the community, the major part of whom have no knowledge or connexion with the arts beyond that which a casual observer may acquire in a rapid visit to Italy, or simply by examination of the most interesting specimens which we have in England.

In the course of my life I have never known anyone who has not been professionally engaged in the study of art, capable of judging of grandeur of style, of composition, of harmony of lines, and of the intricacy of drapery.

At the Academy of St. Luke I have heard the system of competition denounced as being a very bad plan, since the greatest sculptors will generally not enter into competition, because they are constantly employed, nor will they compete with young men unknown to fame. Competition, therefore, only brings forth mediocrity. It is true there are among young sculptors many men of talent, but they have not the necessary experience and practice to perform great works. In the competition for the Wellington monument, not one of the celebrated sculptors of Europe sent in models.

I will here take occasion to mention the mode of proceeding at the Academy of St Luke, when the members have to judge of sculpture and paintings for the prizes. When the models are to be judged the place is filled with the academicians, painters and sculptors, examining the models submitted to them. When the secretary rings his little bell to call the sculptors to their task, all the painters retire and the sculptors are left alone to form their decision upon the models; the latter do not consider that the painters are sufficient judges in their department, and again the painters exclude the sculptors when the former decide upon the paintings submitted for the premiums. Each to his own profession.

The judges upon the models submitted for the Wellington monument had neither sculptors nor painters among them on that important occasion.

From my long experience of the Academy of

St Luke, my conviction is that they discharge their duty with ability and fairness whenever they have to judge of designs laid before them, and they are always tenacious of the honour of their Academy. Often designs from the Roman provinces are sent here to be judged, and I have never heard of any dissatisfaction expressed.

The academicians are composed of Italians principally; there are also a few French, Germans, and one Englishman, that is, myself. At present Cavaliere Tenerani is the President; he was a pupil of Thorwaldsen. I consider him to be the first sculptor now in Europe, and his style is most pure and beautiful, but the works which will consign his name to posterity are chiefly of a religious character, although he has executed some classical subjects which are worthy of the highest commendation, and his portrait statues are of first-rate excellence.

CHAPTER XIV

THE GREEK SCULPTURE AT ROME

My life in Rome has always been a very happy
one, but during that turbulent period of revolu-
tionary agitation we could not pursue our labours;
therefore, those long months of tumult were the
most disagreeable period of my stay at Rome.
When the Pope came back, and Rome returned
to its original state of quietude, we resumed our
delightful labours with renewed pleasure. I read
my books in tranquillity, and I modelled with fresh
pleasure and with revived hopes of producing
better works than I had hitherto done. I renewed
my visits to the Vatican, there refreshing my
spirits in that Pantheon, surrounded by the Gods of
Hellas, her demi-gods and heroes. It is not to criti-
cise that I go there, but to seek instruction in my
art, which the Greeks carried to perfection. Those
few masterpieces which have come down to us,
though I have dwelled upon them thousands of
times, still at every new visit are contemplated by
me with fresh wonder and admiration, such is the

influence which anything perfect both in design and execution has upon the mind. Those grand works of the Greeks are ever new, and always produce fresh enchantment however often they may be surveyed. In order to obtain a correct perception of their merits, and to understand the sublime and beautiful, our taste must be cultivated by long study and great experience. To surpass the best works of the Greeks is a hopeless task ; to approach them is a triumph to the modern artist. How few come near to them !

The greater part of the people who go to the Vatican collection of sculpture spend too much of their time in dwelling upon inferior works—those hard, stiff repetitions ; but the student who has acquired knowledge when he enters the first beautiful gallery called the Braccio Nuovo makes up to the Minerva Medica with the serpent at her feet, spear in her hand, and the helmet on her head That statue is unquestionably, in my opinion, the finest in the Vatican—that is, of the draped class.

The Greeks in their personification of wisdom have given us an image worthy of their Genius and Philosophy Athena is beautiful, but her beauty does not affect the passions; her form is chaste and pure, with an expression of seriousness and reflection ; her attitude is always majestic and grand. The contemplation of such an image purifies and elevates the mind. The Minerva

Medica is one of the greatest favourites of the judges of art; it represents Athena Polias, the guardian goddess of Athens. It is most probably a repetition after Phidias. It was found in the round building on the Esquiline Hill, commonly known by the name of the Temple of Minerva Medica.

A few feet in advance is the great statue of the Nile with a large family of children playing all round about him, those children representing the increase of the river Nile to the height of sixteen cubits. The sixteenth is placed in the cornucopia in his hand to show that fertility was spread over the land. This statue was found near the Church of Santa Maria Sopra Minerva, where anciently stood the Temple of Isis and Serapis, in the pontificate of Leo the Tenth, by whom it was placed in the Vatican. This splendid work of art is not a repetition, but an original production finished by the master himself. It is only the artist who has studied nature who can decide between an original and a copy; here nature is represented full and large, rather exuberant and very fleshy. The head is truly grand, and turns to the left shoulder with a most paternal expression, and the whole is in perfect repose. This great work has no doubt been executed by an artist of no common celebrity, and is a noble study for the student

At the end of the Gallery on the opposite side is the statue of Demosthenes; it is one of the finest I know of, but it is a repetition. The nude part represents rather a lean person, the head is very expressive, and full of character. Let us take a cast of this beautiful statue. Strip it of its drapery, and model upon the figure a coat, trousers, and, without omitting the cravat, all the charm which we now feel in the contemplation of this statue would vanish—to me it would be a disgusting object as a work of art.

Opposite to the Minerva already described is a statue a little larger than life, it is called Modesty (Pudicizia) and is veiled, as she is seen represented on some medals with the inscription Pudicitia. This statue is richly draped, the hand over the head holding the veil is modern and clumsy. It was formerly in the Villa Mattei, and was placed in the Vatican Museum by Clement the Fourteenth (Ganganelli).

We then come to a group of Silenus and infant Bacchus. There is another repetition in the museum at Paris, which is still finer than this in the Braccio Nuovo. Silenus holds in his arms the infant Bacchus, and looks at him with an expression of pleasure and affection; he, as well as the infant, are crowned with ivy, a plant sacred to Bacchus.

Notwithstanding the destruction of Greek art,

we are still in possession of works representing the
different characters in nature, the highest ideal
beauty, the heroic, and down to the more common
nature, such as the rustic, as we see in their Fauns,
Satyrs, and Silenus ; but there is beauty in all
these different characters, it is all collective beauty.
This group, particularly the one in Paris, is a
work of high excellence, and a fine study for the
student.

When we come out of the Braccio Nuovo we
are in the long narrow gallery, Museo Chiaramonte,
which leads us to the Torso.   The principal things
are on our right hand, a fine specimen of flying
drapery, a female figure, headless, in movement.

From thence we come to a very fine head of
Minerva with glass eyes and a helmet, part of
which is antique, and there are small holes, which
proves that the helmet was covered with plates of
gold ; the ears are bored, by which it would appear
that she was intended to be decorated with earrings.   The ears of the Venus de Medicis are also
bored, as well as some other fine antique heads at
Rome.   This invaluable specimen of Greek art in
a perfect state of preservation was found by Mr.
Fagan [1] in the ruins of ancient Laurento.

The finest of the many repetitions which have

---

[1] Robert Fagan (d 1816) the diplomatist   He was a good amateur
portrait painter   He was at this time the British Consul for Sicily
and the Ionian Isles

come down to us of Cupid bending his bow, by
Praxiteles, stood in this place How often did we
dwell upon it ! This beautiful statue is gone—
gone for ever from Rome. Pio Nono has made a
present of it to the Emperor of Russia. In its
place stands another repetition of the same, but
very inferior and not worth much.

Near to the Cupid is a beautiful bust of
Augustus when very young ; the point of the nose
is restored. It was found at Ostia by Mr Fagan,
the British Consul, in the year 1800.

We ascend a few steps to the Vestibule and
there is the torso of Hercules, commonly called Il
Torso di Belvedere. This fragment is esteemed as
one of the finest monuments of Grecian art ; it is,
from the lion's skin on thigh, supposed to represent a Hercules in repose after his labours. It
was so much admired by M. Angelo that he
formed his style upon it. It is one of the few
works which has come down to our time with the
name of the artist inscribed in Greek letters ; on
the front of the rock on which he sits we read,
Apollonius, the son of Nestor the Athenian,
made it. It was found near the Church of
Andrea della Valle, where stood the Theatre of
Pompey.

Then we see the statue of Meleager. I cannot
admire this statue, to me it appears stiff, particularly in the limbs, the head is the best part

of this work.   It was found in a vineyard out of
the Porta Portese, and purchased by Clement
the Fourteenth.

We now come to the Apollo Belvedere, this
celebrated statue which has been admired for
upwards of three centuries in this Museum, and
by the consent of all the best judges considered to
be the finest and most sublime of all the Greek
productions of ideal art which has come down to
our age.   The God is here represented as having
discharged his arrow either at the Python Serpent,
or sending his darts into the camp of the Greeks, as
described by Homer, or it may be against the
impious Giants.   The swelling of the nostrils, and
the disdain on the lip is so delicately touched that
the beauty of his divine countenance is undisturbed.
What judgment this required, and what a specimen
we have here of Greek refinement!   No description
in prose or poetry can impress the mind with
an image of sublimity and beauty as much as this
statue does.   His form is refined to the highest
degree of beauty, even celestial beauty.   The artist
who is not capable of feeling the perfection of this
wonderful statue ought not to be employed in
painting or sculpturing the archangel Michael.
The Apollo was found at Antium, about 24 miles
distant from Rome, a city celebrated in Roman
History from the Palace of the Cæsars, which was
decorated with some of the noblest works of

Greece. This statue was bought by Julius the Second before he ascended the throne, and was placed by him in the Vatican.

The Laocoon This group was estimated in the age of Pliny the Elder as a first-rate production of ancient art, and has been so considered to the present day. The expression of suffering pervades every feature and limb, the management of the composition and treatment of the forms is worthy of the great school of Grecian art. It is the work of three united artists of the School of Rhodes, a father and two sons, Agesander, Polidorus and Athenodorus. The School of Rhodes was very famous about one hundred years before the Christian era. This group was discovered in the baths of Titus in the year 1505.

Mercury. This fine statue known as the Antinous of the Vatican, until the renowned antiquarian Visconti came forth, and for the first time pronounced it to be Mercury; though there was none of his attributes remaining, and it was observed by many persons of note at the time that it could not represent the messenger of the Gods, for the forms were much too robust. But the acute and learned Visconti has satisfied the world that this fine work of art represents Mercury as the presiding God of the Gymnasium, which accounts for his athletic form. Some repetitions have been found which retain parts of the

Caduceus and another which has some portions
of the wings at the ankles. This statue was so
highly esteemed by Nicolas Poussin that he made
it his standard of proportions. It was found in
the baths of Hadrian, near San Martino in Monte,
about three hundred years ago.

Ariadne, abandoned by Theseus in the island of
Naxos. This magnificent statue had long been
known by the name of Cleopatra, owing to the
early antiquarians mistaking the serpent-bracelet
on her arm for the asp, but Visconti settled that
matter for ever. There is no doubt of its representing Ariadne oppressed and fatigued, in her affliction;
she has laid herself down on the shore and sleep
has stolen upon her senses, but it is not the sleep
of a tranquil mind; her attitude suggests restless-
ness, and the upper part of her dress is somewhat
disordered, exposing her lovely bosom, and part of
the body. This statue is in the highest style of
art and admirably composed—so natural and so
graceful. The contemplation of this grand work is
always a new pleasure and ever will be. It was
placed by Julius the Second in the Vatican, and is
one of the first placed there. It is not known
where it was found. The sarcophagus on which it
stands describes a subject rarely met with, the war
of the Giants

Apollo Sauroctonos. The original was in bronze
by Praxiteles and mentioned by Pliny. There are

several copies of this most beautiful and graceful statue come down to us, and one in bronze in the Villa Albani smaller than those which we have in marble. The forms of this figure are refined to the highest degree of beauty and delicacy, and the composition is in accordance with the laws of art, which laws we learn from the Greeks. The left arm leaning on the tree is extended forward, whilst the foot on the same side retreats back, the right arm forms an angle over the straight standing leg, and the head gracefully turns over the highest shoulder. This arrangement produces balance, grace, and perfect harmony throughout the whole, at the same time being natural and easy. This repetition was found on the Palatine Hill, in the year 1777.

In the same gallery with Aridane we come to a very great favourite, ordinarily called "Il Genio del Vaticano." It is a half-figure of Cupid, but this is a grown-up youth.

There exist two other repetitions of the same. One of my greatest delights is to contemplate this fragment It is impossible to imagine a countenance more lovely, pure, serene and spiritually beautiful How luxuriant are his waving locks round his soft neck! and the inclined position of the head is graceful and chaste. I have no doubt that this statue represents celestial Cupid, and Visconti believes it to be after Praxiteles.

Leaving celestial Eros with reluctance, and after passing some fine works we are riveted by a grand and beautiful statue of an Amazon. The lover of sculpture is here struck by the power of the Greek artists in blending severity of character and strength with the female form; the face is grave, and seems as if incapable of tender emotion, yet beautiful. The shoulders are somewhat broad, and the left breast which is exposed, is small, not prominent. The arms and limbs are particularly fine. The tunic is a specimen of the dress which the Amazons are supposed to have worn, which is in numerous crisp folds and gives breadth to the flesh. The style of this statue is worthy of the School of Phidias. Visconti believes that the tunic was painted because it is darker than the flesh. Since the time of Visconti many fragments have been found with colours on them. Close to the last statue mentioned are those of Menandros and Poseidippos sitting in chairs. They are admirable specimens of portrait statues, so truthful to nature in character and action.

Opposite to the fragment of celestial Cupid already mentioned, is a statue of a young Faun, resting with his bent arm on the trunk of a tree, holding a pipe in his hand. He has left off playing, and there is mirth and good-nature in his youthful face, though a rustic he is full of

beauty The whole figure is in perfect ease,
and the relaxed leg and foot are beautifully
negligent, suitable to his character. The longer
we look at this admirable statue, the more we
are convinced with Visconti, that this is a copy
from the celebrated Faun by Praxiteles; the
repetitions of it are numerous, but this one is
the finest of them all. When several copies of
the same work have been found, it is reasonable
to suppose that the original must have been
celebrated. There exist four or five repetitions of
the Venus of Praxiteles, and also about the same
number from his Apollo Sauroctonos—one is in
bronze in the Villa Albani.

We shall now enter a small circular room, the
architecture of which is very elegant and rich, the
ceiling is painted with subjects and the mosaic floor
is antique. There are a few fine works here, but
the one which gives me particular pleasure is the
crouching Venus. It may be a Nymph at the
Bath. This statue is so fleshy and beautiful that I
am inclined to consider it an original work and not
a repetition. There are others to be found else-
where of the same statue but not so fine as this
one

Among the vast numbers of ancient statues that
have come down to us, very few are those represented in a doubled up or crouching attitude,
such positions are never favourable to the display

of beauty and the long graceful lines, nor are the
proportions seen to advantage. The figure is here
natural, but both arms form angles, as well as the
limbs which cover all the front of the body. Still,
we admire this great favourite.

Walking through the small round room of the
nine Muses and their leader, Apollo Musegetes, we
enter the great Rotonda which contains large
statues of high merit. On our right as we enter is
a colossal statue of Jove, a sublime production,
upon which we may meditate a little. The Pagan
Greeks represented the divinity under human form,
and so we see God painted and sculptured in the
Catholic churches. This image produced by the
Pagan artist strikes us with the idea of the highest
sublimity and beauty—beauty unfading. The
expression is paternal, venerable, still ever young.
How rich are his ambrosial locks! Power,
benevolence, majesty, and beauty are combined in
this Greek work. Let us now turn our eyes to
the image of God by the Christian artists; he is
represented by them as a venerable aged man, with
vigour and action, but time has diminished his
beauty: you feel that he is on the decline of age—
he is a grand old man and nothing more.

The Greek artists were enlightened by the
philosophers; the Gods of the wise men personified
by the sculptors were pure, passionless, and divinely
beautiful. The poets also made them beautiful

and mighty, but with mortal propensities and sensations. Ares roared aloud with pain, and Aphrodite suffered from the pain in her hand when wounded.

Our artistic ambition becomes often depressed in the contemplation of these wonderful works. In the art of sculpture, the Greeks were Gods. We, with all our efforts, feel it hard toil to creep upwards after them. Though the eminence upon which they stood is beyond our reach, still, the sculptor duly imbued with the principles of his art— who has received the gift of genius—who is ambitious of future fame, toils on, and feels delight in his labours. The study of the beautiful is his profession; if he pursues the true path, he will find all that is best calculated to elevate his art. In the Vatican we go from statue to statue, from fragment to fragment, like the bee from flower to flower How delightful to dwell upon the charming Discobolus of Naucides of Argos; the original is lost, but this in the round room of the Biga is the best of all existing repetitions. This beautiful work is admired for the natural action and the graceful play of all its movements, and for its broad style and beautiful proportions He is in the act of judging the distance before throwing his discus. In this composition neither of the arms cross the body. The moment of the action represented permits

M

the exposure of the figure in front, it is the most favourable for the display of beauty and long flowing lines; such is the arrangement in the Apollo and most of the fine statues.

In the same room we see the Discobolus of Myron, which is mentioned by the Greek writers. It has been frequently remarked that a man could not remain in such a posture; this represents however a momentary movement and is perfectly true to nature, and the sculptor must have often seen the action of throwing the discus. The modern head of this repetition turns from the discus, but the one in the Palazzo Massimo is the most valuable, the head having remained entire, and turns back towards the discus.

In this room also is a statue of Bacchus of beautiful execution, which shews in great perfection his double character, that is, a combination of the male and female form A Greek writer says that when the God appeared among the males, he looked like a girl, but when he was among the females he appeared like a boy, such was the delicate feminine form given to Dionysos, son of Love and Beauty.

From the room of the Biga, turning on the right and going through the iron gate, we are in a long gallery full of statues and fragments. Those who are capable of judging may trace the great original mind in a very mediocre performance. This is a basso-relievo upon the front of a sarcophagus which stands upon our left as we proceed. It represents the destruction of Niobe and her children; Apollo and Diana are seen discharging their fatal arrows upon them, and Niobe may be seen holding her youngest daughter to her lap, and with her left hand raising her mantle to shield her child. Her action is dignified in the midst of all this scene of terror, wild despair, the dying and the dead—all her own children. In this work we see grandeur of conception, and fine composition; the action of every figure is true to nature. The original must have been the production of a great master and in the best period of art.

Also here is another sarcophagus upon which is sculptured in basso-relievo, a most tragical event, so renowned in Greek myth. This also must be the conception of a great artist. The subject is Orestes, assisted by his friend Pylades, whilst inflicting the punishment of death upon his mother, Clytemnestra, for the murder of his father Agamemnon. Orestes was destined by Fate and commanded by the Oracle to execute this unnatural act. It having been likewise decreed that Pylades at the same time should slay Egistheus, the seducer of Clytemnestra. Orestes obeyed the commands of the Oracle, and his obedience to the divine will brought upon him instant punishment, the dreadful Furies perpetually persecuting him even to madness. At last he received mercy and was restored to peace. There is an antique repetition of this same work in the wall of a house here, also one in the cortile of the Palazzo Giustiniani.

CHAPTER XV

ANTIQUE SCULPTURE AT ROME

As I delight in bassi-relievi, I will now pay a visit to the Capitol and re-examine a fine sarcophagus upon which is cut a basso-relievo representing a battle of the Amazons with the Greeks. The composition is fine and full of animation and masterly grouping. The portion on our left as we look at the work was selected and drawn by Flaxman, and at his lectures shown to the students as a specimen of the beautiful concatenation of the lines composing arms and legs. In this particular Flaxman was very clever, as we observe in his admirable compositions.

Here we admire a fine basso-relievo of Endymion asleep whilst his faithful dog is on the watch—it is by a great master.

We have at Rome hundreds of alti and bassi-relievi but inferior sculpture The study of the reliefs of the Elgin marbles enables us now to distinguish the pure style of this part of

sculpture from the corrupt. the degenerate. We
have scarcely any specimens at Rome of the chaste
flat manner of the Athenian school   In the Villa
Albani there is, over one of the fire-places, a
very fine flat basso-relievo.   It represents Orpheus,
Eurydice, and Mercury ; there is a repetition of it
at Naples.   We have also a pure specimen at
Grotta Ferrata representing a beardless Philosopher
in a sitting posture ; it is in alto-relievo, but at the
same time flat, a most valuable specimen.   I
believe Sir C. Eastlake had a cast of it sent to
England.   It is also interesting, being found at
the spot where. it is supposed, stood Cicero's villa.
I must not forget to name an alto-relievo in the
Villa Albani of Antinous over one of the chimney-
pieces—it is perfectly beautiful, and I think that
Winkelmann considered it equal to the Apollo for
style ; the execution of the hair is perfect.   Here
is also a large alto-relievo, figures nearly life-size, a
young hero on the ground defending himself whilst
the victor is giving him a blow with his sword, and
at the same time holding his horse, for he is
mounted.   This work is pure Athenian.

Returning to statues, the Capitol contains a
noble study for the artist ; it is a statue representing a dying barbarian soldier (called the Dying
Gladiator).   We perceive in this statue an original
work, not a repetition, by a great master—but
there is no name upon it.   Common nature is here

admirably modelled, and the head with high cheek bones, short flat nose and moustache; the Greeks represented the Barbarians as less beautiful than themselves. The action of this figure, so natural, is at the same time full of variety from the arrangement of all its parts. It tells its own tale, and affects you at once—as you gaze upon him, sympathy creeps over your senses. He bleeds— his life flows slowly away—silent and calm—he is fast sinking—will faint and die. I have heard some people say that Greek sculpture wants expression—they want perception and feeling.

This statue has many more admirers than the Apollo Belvedere among the English, which proves that the sublime and the most refined beauty does not so quickly impress the mass of people. To enjoy the divine beauty of the Apollo, taste must be highly cultivated, but how few are cultivated in high art, those who are, participate in a higher degree of mental enjoyment than those who have not studied the first principle of art. In the same room is a fine portrait statue of Zeno; this figure is a remarkable specimen of the imitation of common nature, and the drapery is very good. There is also a large bust greatly admired, it goes under the name of Ariadne, but it is, as Winkelmann says, Dionysos. The statue called Flora is a fine specimen of drapery. In the next room we admire the statue of an Amazon, it is a repetition, the

same as the one in the Vatican, the original must
have been a first-rate work.   In this room there are
two statues of centaurs, small, in black marble: they
are of high excellence and were found in the villa
of Adrian   They are the works of Papia and
Aristea, their names are cut in Greek on the
marble.

Here is a group of a child playing with a swan,
there is also a repetition of it in the Vatican.   This
little group is very clever in composition and very
natural, the plump boy has his arms tight round
the neck of the swan, pulling it back with all his
might. whilst the bird is pushing itself forward,
which gives contrary action, variety, and great
animation to the whole—the struggle is great on
both sides.   Winkelmann thinks that this group is
not by a great Greek artist, because they would
not condescend to copy infantine forms, which are
nothing more than lumps of fat.   The great
sculptors of this day rarely sculpture fat children;
statues of babies are subjects only for women to
admire, which they always do.   Painters of
eminence have enriched their pictures with the
representation of the infantine forms.

In the next room we are struck with admiration
of the sitting statue of Agrippina, wife of
Germanicus and mother of Caligula   Can we
contemplate the noble representation of this lady
without remembering her end ?   She was banished

by Tiberius to the island of Pandataria; upon her reviling him for it, he caused a centurion to beat out one of her eyes; when she resolved to starve herself to death, he ordered her mouth to be forced open, and meat to be crammed down her throat But she persisted in her resolution, and died soon afterwards.[1] Canova could not resist adopting the noble, natural and graceful attitude of this figure in his portrait statue of Napoleon's mother, which is in the collection of the Duke of Devonshire.

In this collection there is another Amazon, different from the two mentioned. She is wounded under the right breast, and with her left hand she presses the wound with part of her dress— how natural is the action of the raising up of the right arm to enable her to see the wound whilst she looks down to it, the situation of which renders it difficult of examination. There is one similar in the Vatican. The collection of busts in the Capitol is very rich, and most interesting.

The collection of sculpture in the Villa Ludovisi is small. The principal work there is a large group representing a barbarian chief in the act of killing himself after having put his wife to death. She is just breathing her last. He is still holding her whilst she is sinking on her knees, with her drooping head and closing eyes, and it would appear as

[1] Suetonius Vita Tiberii, lii

if she had received death at the hands of her
husband with resignation. This scene is supposed
to take place on the field of battle—the hero is
vanquished. This work has been called Paetus
and Arria.

I will venture to say that there is a fault in the
composition of this group, which consists in the
manner of raising the hand in order to plunge the
weapon into his throat—this action hides the face
of the man from those who are looking at the work
in front. It is a law in this species of composition
that the front view of the group shall be as perfect
as possible, uninterrupted and not cut up by
crossing arms or parts; as in this case the face is
partly hid from the spectator by the uplifted arm,
the law in question is greatly infringed upon.
We know that groups in the round cannot be
equally perfect in all views. The most difficult
thing in our art is the composition of a group,
few great sculptors will attempt it except, indeed,
the inexperienced

A sculptor in London, who had great admirers.
made a group which was greatly eulogised—it consisted of six horses and six men, a towering group
—here we have twenty-four horses' legs, twelve
arms and twelve legs, which makes forty-eight
members to arrange—nothing but confusion can
result from such a number of parts; such an
attempt proves the author to have been ignorant

of the first principles of his art. The uncultivated cannot comprehend all the difficulties which attend a composition of this character—such is the result of the imperfect acquaintance with this intricate sort of composition My observations apply only to sculpture and not to painting.

The next group we admire is that of a woman conversing with a youth younger than herself; the female has her hair cut short, which is a sign of mourning—on that account they say that it represents Electra and Orestes; the drapery is very good and the form of the youth is in fine style.

People admire the statue of a young man sitting, grasping his bent knee and sword with both hands. It is supposed to represent Mars, Cupid is crouched at his foot; the sculpture is fine and the countenance noble and beautiful.

The colossal head of Juno in Greek marble is highly admired for its divine beauty—the nose has never been injured, which is rare in an antique statue. This splendid work of Greek art is a most valuable study. There are in this valuable collection other statues of great interest and value. There is also a modern group, life-size, representing Pluto carrying off Proserpine; it is the work of the Cavalier Bernini. To see this group, which is a good specimen of the master, by the side of the pure Greek statues is valuable to the artist; it is like seeing Vice and Virtue in juxtaposition.

After my delightful wanderings in the Vatican,
Capitol, Villa Albani, and the Villa Ludovisi, I
return to my studio in the Via Fontanella, having
quenched, as I constantly do, my thirst at the pure
fountain of Hellas. My mind is more and more
inspired by the immortal works which I have been
contemplating; it is by constant meditation upon
such productions that I feel the dignity of my
delightful art and the ambition of fame kept up
with ever stirring melody.

> "The thirst of Fame is the parent of excellence"

> "I, too, will strive o'er earth my flight to raise,
>   And winged by Victory, catch the gale of praise"

The praise of the living is very encouraging, at
the same time we know that inferior performances
often meet with admiration, artists of very moderate
abilities often meet with great patronage. That
praise which I most pant for is the one which I am
never destined to hear, for it is that which
posterity may give. He who has acquired by
constant labour a true knowledge of nature and
the antique, with genius for invention, and can
regulate his imagination within the bounds of
nature's laws—who labours more for the love of
glory than for the love of gain—may hope that his
name will live in his works when his body is mixed
up with the earth.

CHAPTER XVI

THE BRAVO'S VISIT—QUEEN VICTORIA'S STATUE FOR THE HOUSES OF PARLIAMENT

ONE day, sitting in my studio looking over my book of designs, I heard a knocking at the street door. I rose and opened the door—there stood a man asking permission to speak to me; he entered and put a letter into my hand; at once I considered him a beggar—I had made up my mind to be uncharitable. The man was well dressed. I opened the letter and saw there were only five or six lines, which I read. I give it in English, having no copy of the letter, which I immediately returned to the writer; the letter ran as follows :—

" I am a man of courage, and capable of running the risk of shedding my blood in executing anything which may concern you, and for a moderate reward I am capable of keeping any secret; full confidence may be placed in me."

" Did you write this?" I said to the man. He was an assassin, and ready, for a moderate sum, to

stab or kill any one that might be offensive to me.
As I was alone and no one near, I began to fear,
thinking, perhaps, he had come to stab me; but I
had not offended any one, nor was I making love to
the nymph of another, nor had I any enemy whom
I wished to be killed on my account. This is the
only instance of an assassin offering his services to
me during my life in Rome.

The streets of Rome are nearly empty of the
natives at an early hour in the evening. One night
a friend of mine, a Roman painter of merit, told me
that he was going to his home along the Corso
about twelve o'clock, when his attention was
arrested by a faint voice crying for help; he saw a
man lying full length in the middle of the street,
and he instantly went up to him, and the man said,
"I am stabbed and I cannot move;" he was faint
from loss of blood, and was afraid that if a carriage
passed it might run over him; "Pray, Signore, to
drag me to the footpath." My friend instantly
took hold of his ankles and dragged him on the side
path, then walked off as quick as possible. "Why
did you leave him so?" said I. He then explained
that if he had been seen with the wounded man,
and that if he should expire there, he would be
arrested, and probably kept a considerable time to
be examined; to avoid such an annoyance he
instantly fled.

I will now return to my own works. First I

will state that the statue of the Queen, mentioned
already, having given satisfaction in high quarters,
I was written to and informed that it was intended
to put a statue of H M. in the new Parliament
House, to stand in a recess in the Prince's Chamber.
I was informed that it was wished that I should
turn my thoughts to the subject. The original
idea was a single statue, but Prince Albert justly
considered the recess much too wide for a single
figure—he was right; and H.R.II. proposed to
add two appropriate allegorical statues, so as to
make an important group. The design which I
sent from Rome represented H.M. sitting upon
her throne with her sceptre in her left hand, and
a laurel crown in her right—the emblem of reward
bestowed upon merit. On her right hand is
Wisdom, and on her left is Justice; these figures
stand lower than the Queen so as to form a
pyramid—certain geometrical forms are necessary
in composition. After my design had been considered, H.R II. suggested that the emblematic
figures should be Justice and Clemency, as the
sovereign is a lady. I was pleased with this idea,
as well as all others entitled to give an opinion
on the subject, so it was adopted. It was intimated to me by letter that if I undertook this
important monument it was considered necessary
that I should come to England, so as to be face
to face with the architect, to fix the dimensions

of the statues to fit the recess in the Prince's
Chamber.   I went to England, and on my arrival
there Sir C. Barry gave me a small room in the
Parliament House to make my sketch model and
then fixed the size of the statues for me.   I
finished my model in one month.   Prince Albert,
who had watched my progress, came with three
or four of the ministers to look at my work, and
H.R.H. praised it to them.   The Royal Commission had a meeting.   The Prince President
was at Osborne with the Queen, and Lord John
Russell took the chair.   I was told that he handed
a note which went round the table, every one
read it—that note was from the Prince expressing
his entire approbation of my model.   All then
voted for the design and that it should be executed
by me.   I was not bound to time—a necessity to
which I feel the greatest disinclination to subject
myself—but I promised to begin the work soon
after my arrival at Rome, and I completed the
monument within five years   It is now put up
in the Prince's Chamber, and there it receives a
fine light, which is of the first importance to
sculpture.   Sir C. Barry proportioned the statues
well for the size of that room—the large dimensions of the statues give a very imposing effect.
I am happy my work is so well seen.

I will venture to make a remark upon my own
work, although it may subject me to the charge

H.M. QUEEN VICTORIA

of vanity, but I do so out of regard to the interests of artists in England and to the advancement in general of art in that country.

I think that monument of the Queen is an important performance for the consideration of all the home-bred sculptors of England—it is a specimen from the Roman school, that great college to which, as I have already stated, all the governments of Europe send their pensioned students, England excepted, in that work I have aimed at the highest style of monumental art—severe simplicity, rich and broad drapery with correctness of outline throughout the whole. This "grandiosa maniera" can only be imbibed at Rome. I was requested to write a description of my work to be printed for the people to read when they are surveying the monument, and I wrote the following. "In the Prince's Chamber is represented, in marble, her most Gracious Majesty Queen Victoria, sitting upon the throne, holding her sceptre, and a laurel crown, that is governing and rewarding: the laurel crown may be considered an emblem of the honour conferred upon intellect and valour. The back of the throne is surmounted by lions, expressive of British strength and courage, and the footstool is adorned by sea-horses to signify dominion upon the ocean: the horse is an emblem of war. On the right of the sovereign stands Justice, on the left Clemency. The former holds the sword and

N

balance : round her neck is suspended the image of Truth. The expression of Justice is inflexible, whilst that of clemency is full of sympathy and sadness—sad for the constant sins which come to her knowledge, but with lenity she keeps the sword sheathed, and offers the olive branch, the sign of peace. Upon the front of the pedestal is a bas-relief of Commerce. Upon the right side is Science, designated by a youth pondering over Geometry : and upon the left a figure denoting the usual arts : in the background are represented a steam engine, the telegraph wire, and other useful objects."

Plato says, " All-seeing Justice; the eye of Justice penetrates into the darkness which conceals the Truth ! " In Egypt the judge, when pronouncing the sentence of death, put on his neck a small image of Truth : it was of Gold. Clemency must have the power of punishment, therefore she is represented with a sword.

The figures are colossal—that of her Majesty being eight feet high, and those of the attendant ones about seven.

CHAPTER XVII

THE TINTED VENUS—PANDORA

WHEN Mr. Joseph Neeld came to Rome he often visited my studio, and at length expressed a wish to possess a statue by me—the subject to be a Venus, nude, but with some drapery modestly arranged without sacrificing too much the form. After Mr. Neeld's departure this subject began to occupy my thoughts by day and by night, as all the works which I have executed have done. Venus has often been the subject of various artists Frequently the first idea of the young is to produce something original—something new, so they give certain airs and twist the figure about, the result is that the simple action of nature vanishes, so you have indeed something new, but it is novelty at a dear cost. This feeling would appear to prevail sometimes among French students in sculpture, and when I visited England after my long absence I observed an inclination of the same kind The instruction which I received saved me from such a

mistake, and led me to the constant attention to
the movements of living beings.

With respect to the statue of the goddess of
beauty and love, I knew that a standing position is
the most favourable for the display of the figure, as
it affords long flowing lines. As to the attitude, I
had often remarked the ladies, when holding in
their hands a fan or some light object of the kind,
generally place their hands in repose in front of the
body—thus my Venus stands with the golden
apple. From her left arm hangs her garment to
the ground, but this is not merely a piece of
drapery, I cut—as a model for the drapery—out the
tunic-mantle (Chitonophoros) which the Greek
ladies wore; this mantle is so arranged that it covers
modestly the figure—not drawn as if on purpose to
conceal, but falls accidentally. So I completed
my Venus to the satisfaction of Mr. Neeld.

A youth from Liverpool came to Rome, Mr.
Preston, with his most amiable young wife, she
draws the figure and paints with considerable
talent. They decided on having a repetition of my
Venus. This repetition I kept on hand five years,
working upon the marble whenever I felt disposed,
and referring often to nature. This second marble
statue is the most laboured work I ever made—it is
superior to the first; the outlines I have endeavoured
to purify up to the highest ideal. As I laboured
on, ever panting for perfection, I fixed so many

degrees of the circle for the convex forms, and the fewer the degrees the more refined and soft the undulating lines became. I copy the following from Winckelmann. "The forms of a beautiful body are determined by lines the centre of which is constantly changing, and which, if continued, would never describe circles. They are, consequently, more simple but also more complex, than a circle, which, however large or small it may be, always has the same centre, and either includes others or is included in others. This diversity was sought after by the Greeks in works of all kinds; and their discernment of its beauty led them to introduce the same system even into the form of their utensils and vases, whose easy and elegant outline is drawn after the same rule; that is, by a line which must be found by means of several circles, so all these works have an elliptical figure and herein consists their beauty. The greater unity there is in the junction of the forms, and in the flowing of one out of another, so much the greater is the beauty of the whole."

The expression which I have attempted to give to my Venus is that of purity and sweetness, with an air of unaffected dignity and grace, and spiritual elevation of character; when our aim is high some allowance must be made if we occasionally fail.

"In great attempts 'tis glorious e'en to fall"

I have alluded already to Polychromy, and I

now return to this important subject again. "It
was as though through Polychromy the ancients
gave expression to the brighter and more ethereal
impulses of the mind. Polychromy was the link
connecting the forms of matter with the airy
fancies in which genius was rife."

When my Venus was finished, I then decorated
her in a manner never seen before in these times.
The flesh tinted like warm ivory (scarcely red),
the eyes blue, the hair blonde, the net which
contains the hair behind is of gold. "And her
fair locks are woven up in gold" (Spenser). The
blue fillets winding round the head are edged
with gold, and she has earrings; her armlet is
also gold, likewise the apple in her hand, which
has a Greek inscription on it: "To the most
beautiful." The drapery is left the white colour
of the marble, the border ornament is in pink
and blue. Upon the back of the tortoise at her
feet is a Greek inscription: "Gibson made me
at Rome."

When all my long labour was complete, I
often sat down in quiet before my work, meditating
upon it and consulting my own simple feelings
I endeavoured to keep myself free from self-
delusion as to the effect of the colouring, which
I put to the test of reason. I said to myself:
'Here is a little nearer approach to the life, therefore more impressive—yes, yes, indeed she seems

an ethereal being with her blue eyes looking upon me.' I forgot at moments that I was gazing at my own production. There sat I before her long and often. How can I ever part with her!

I am convinced that the Greek taste was right in colouring their sculpture—the warm glow is most agreeable to the feeling, and so is the variety obtained by it. The flesh is one tone, the hair another, the colouring of the eyes gives animation, and the drapery has its colour and all the ornaments are distinctly seen—all these are great advantages.

The moderns, being less refined than the Greeks in matters of art, are, from stupid custom, reconciled to the white statue. The flesh is white, the hair is white, the eyes are white, and the drapery white: this monotonous cold object of art is out of harmony with everything which surrounds it.

It is not necessary that I should give here quotations from the classic authors touching upon their Polychromatic practice; all these are published, as well as the fragments found with some traces of colour. Those who think that the Greeks did not colour sculpture in the high period of art are grossly mistaken. The Greek public were accustomed to see sculpture in gold and ivory, and the eyes in glass and precious stones—a cold white statue would therefore have appeared incomplete to those people. Leaving out Greek authorities, I can say now that the effect of colour delicately applied and with judgment charms me   All the sculptors in Rome and the painters, including Cornelius agree with me, also Visconti : but the sculptors said : we dare not follow your example for fear we might not sell our works.   I said to them, " I will fight it out with them and go on "

When his Grace the Duke of Northumberland was here, he came often to my studio.   One day he said to me, " If you could keep the Venus in Rome for a considerable time, she would be visited by travellers of different nations, and they would spread her fame for you "

I have now kept my Venus at Rome for four years after being finished, and I may say truly that in the period mentioned she has been looked at by several hundred persons of different nations, the English included.   I think I may name the following personages who came in the course of one winter : The Grand Duchess Olga, and, in a few days after, her Imperial Majesty the Dowager Empress of Russia, with her numerous train, the Grand Duchess Helena, the two Kings of Bavaria, the Prince of Prussia, H.R.H. the Count of Syracuse, and lately her Imperial Highness the Duchess Leuchtenberg.

From time to time, I received letters of complaints from Mrs. Preston for not sending the Venus home.   She felt, as time advanced, that I

was not using her well. In her last angry letter
she put a simple question to me which I was to
answer: " Are you using me well or ill? " I
replied: " I am using you abominably bad, and I
confess my sin, but the fact is I cannot screw up
my courage and send away my Goddess: it is as
difficult for me to part with her as it would be for
Mr Preston to part with you. I will now copy
some verses for you upon the Venus, written by
the Rev. Edward Stokes, hoping that this poetry
will keep you a little quieter for some time to
come.

> "Oh pure Ideal of the perfect Grace
>   That is in woman ! Such a form as thine
> In glorious Hellas did young Fancy trace,
>   Till beauties more than human seemed divine
>
> In such a form—seeking her destined home
>   On high Olympus, from the azure wave
> Rose Aphrodite—daughter of the foam—
>   The hearts of Gods and mortals to enslave
>
> In such a form—to win the glittering prize
>   By Discord's hand amid the fairest thrown
> Unveiled before the Trojans' dazzling eyes
>   She claimed the palm of Beauty for her own
>
> Oh wondrous might of Genius to inspire
>   The lifeless marble with a living ray
> Flashed from the source of its own genial fire,
>   Which lights the Poet's heart with endless day
>
> Oh ! touch of art ennobling ! who can gaze
>   Upon that matchless form—that modest mien,
> Nor feel thy power his inmost thoughts to raise
>   Nor learn to reverence purity serene?"

I have lived to the year 1859, having practised
my art in Rome forty-two years, and I can truly

say that it is still the delight of my soul, and
occupies all my thoughts. To be riding my own
hobby-horse in the clear atmosphere of Rome
is to me the greatest felicity, nor is this happiness
ever disturbed by the pangs of envy towards others
who are in the race with me. Theophrastus says,
" The envious are more unhappy than others in
this respect, that they are troubled, not only at
their misfortune, but also at the good fortune of
others."

I will continue to relate my artistic proceedings.
In the year 1856 his Grace the Duke of Wellington
and his amiable Duchess visited the " Eternal
City," and they often came to see my works in the
Via Fontanella.

The Duke expressed a wish to possess my Venus,
but she was not disposable. A little before his
Grace's departure from Rome he intimated to me
his wish that I should execute for him some
coloured statue, and he proposed the subject—it
was Pandora. He then pointed out to me how he
would like it to be represented, which was the
moment when she comes to life and seeming to be
conscious of existence; nude, with some drapery
hanging from her arm. I expressed my apprehen-
sion that the subject so treated would not be
sufficiently understood by those who surveyed it.
Let a box be placed at her feet, said the Duke,
let her hands be open in an attitude of surprise at

the discovery of her new existence. At once I saw that his Grace had imbibed an erroneous impression respecting the best mode of treating the statue which he wished to have executed, and I then said to him that I would model a Pandora.

The conception of a subject is the first and most important part of our art, and he who has the greatest genius is the most likely to succeed in it.

Although the myth of Pandora is so well known, I may here run over the story, as it will impress us with what is necessary in treating the statue.

. . . "And now the crippled artist God
Illustrious, moulded from the yielding clay
A bashful virgin's image, as advised
Saturnian Jove   Then Pallas azure-ey'd
Bound with the zone her bosom, and with robe
Of silvery whiteness decked her folded limbs ;
With her own hands a variegated veil
Placed on her head, all marvellous to sight
Twined with her tresses a delicious wreath
Of mingled verdure, and fresh-blooming flowers ;
And clasped her brow with diadem of gold
Thus Vulcan with his glorious hands had framed
Elaborate, pleasing to the Sire of Gods,
Full many works of curious craft, to sight
Wondrous, He grav'd thereon, full many beasts
Of Earth, and of fishes of the rolling main
Of these innumerable he there had wrought,
And elegance of Art there shone profuse
And admirable e'en as though they mov'd
In my life, and utter'd animal sounds

*   *   *   *   *

By Jove's design arose the bashful maid ;
The cestus Pallas clasp'd, the robe arrayed,
Ador'd Persuasion and the Graces young
Her taper'd limbs with golden jewels hung

Round her fair brows the lovely-tressèd hours
A garland twined of spring's purpureal flow'rs
The whole attire Minerva's graceful art
Dispos'd, adjusted, form'd to every part "[1]

It is evident that the best moment of time to represent Pandora is when she is all attired by the blue-eyed goddess, Minerva, assisted by the Graces and reverend Persuasion, and crowned with flowers by the lovely Hours—also the gold diadem made and presented by Vulcan.

I have represented Pandora as described by Hesiod, and with the fatal box in her hand, drooping her head in deep thought; her eyes are turned a little from the box, whilst her hand is ready to raise the lid. The figure is still and motionless, but the mind is in full activity, labouring under the harassing feelings of intense curiosity and fear and perplexity. Her thoughts have dwelled too long upon the box. Pandora is already lost —we are the sufferers, but Hope did not escape with the evil brood, she was shut in, and remains to the last with us.

When modelling this charming subject I roused up my ideas to the highest degree. As I advanced towards the finishing of the clay, often I thought to myself, what would Praxiteles think of this work? What is there that he would condemn—is the sentiment pure and refined—is there elevation

---

[1] Hesiod. *The Theogony*, ll 759–778. *Works and Days*, ll. 101–108 Gibson has used Elton's version

of character—are the forms and the drapery purely Athenian? In what estimation will posterity hold this work of mine—will it be an honour to my name which is engraved upon it in Greek characters? How I wish that I had been born in the days of Praxiteles! I am a Welshman, but with a soul ever panting after the perfection of the immortal sculptors of Hellas.

The following is applicable to the ambitious artist:—" If ever, therefore, we are engaged in a work which requires a grandeur of style and exalted sentiments, would it not then be of use to raise in ourselves such reflections as these: How in this case would Homer or Plato or Demosthenes have raised their thoughts? Or, if it be historical: How would Thucydides? For these celebrated persons, being proposed by us for our pattern and imitation, will in some degree lift up our souls to the standard of their own genius. It will be yet of greater use if to the preceding reflections we add these: What would Homer or Demosthenes have thought of this piece? Or, what judgment would they have passed upon it?"[1]

Before the model of my Pandora was finished, numbers of people came to see it every day, and Lady Marion Alford watched its progress with great interest. A little before her Ladyship's departure from Rome, I said to her that I had

[1] Longinus On the Sublime, Cap. XIV.

not felt quite sure that the Duke of Wellington would be disposed to take the statue, as I had departed altogether from his idea of treating the subject. Her Ladyship then said to me, " In that case may I be the possessor of your Pandora ? "

As the heat of Rome was increasing, I left it for England, taking with me three photographs of the Pandora. When I arrived in London, I waited upon the Duke of Wellington. On seeing the photographs, he said. " Well, I am now convinced of the truth of what some of my friends said to me who were at Rome and saw your model ; they said that you had produced a beautiful figure, but," said he, " you have not followed my own idea." " No, I have treated the subject according to *my* own idea." " You are very stubborn." " Duke, I am a Welshman, and all the world knows that we are a stubborn race."

Before my departure for Rome, I received the following letter from the Duke of Wellington :

" *October* 12*th*, 1856.

" MY DEAR MR. GIBSON,

"Somehow or other, I have missed your departure if you are gone. I wanted finally to tell you that, much as I admire the design of your Pandora, it reminds me always of my original notion and causes a disappointment which does an injustice to the statue. I think, therefore, that if it does not inconvenience you, which is not likely, as I hear nothing but admiration of it, you had better not consider that it is intended for me. However, somehow or other, I must have a great work of yours at Apsley House.

"Yours most sincerely,
"WELLINGTON."

I wrote the following :—

"MY LORD DUKE,

"I beg to offer your Grace many thanks for the favour of your kind note. I leave England for Rome on the 17th inst.

"I shall always remember with pleasure that I am indebted to you for having proposed to me the subject of Pandora for a coloured statue. Everybody agrees that it is a good subject, but I feel with you that my design does not correspond with the idea of the moment of time and the mode of representation which your Grace had conceived of the subject, therefore it would not give you the same pleasure. Permit me to assure you that your not having the statue will not inconvenience me, for Lady Marion Alford often came to see the progress of the model in clay, and one day I told her Ladyship that I was not sure that you would be satisfied with the work, as it did not correspond with your own idea of treating the subject. Her

Ladyship then said that in case your Grace might
not wish to have the Pandora, she made me promise
that she should be the owner, and she added that
if the statue should fall to her lot, she would have
a proper place made for it, so now I will write to
her Ladyship.   Permit me also to add that I shall
always entertain very pleasing and grateful feelings
towards your Grace and the Duchess for kindness
to me at Rome and in England.

    " I have the honour to be

      " My Lord Duke,

   " Your Grace's most obedient servant,

         " JOHN GIBSON."

Lady Marion Alford became an admirer of
Polychromy, and she has ordered me to colour
the Pandora for her, which I shall do, and hope to
produce a beautiful effect : this will be my third
coloured statue.

I have had the advantage of being acquainted
with this lady from her youth at Rome, and cannot
resist the satisfaction of adding my feeble tribute
to that of others with reference to the great merit
of her studies in copying from the old masters and
producing original compositions, which practice,
having been long pursued, has given her correct
judgment in painting and sculpture

During my visit to England, the Duchess of
Wellington one day expressed her desire to have

her bust modelled by me. Her Grace said that Marochetti ill-made a bust of her, which did not give satisfaction, and then added that he modelled a second which was not more successful than the first. I could not help observing at the first glance what a fine subject I had before me, so I eagerly complied with the desire expressed by her Grace, and, as I surveyed her fine countenance, I felt certain of success.

I began the model of the bust at Apsley House, and, after a few sittings, I allowed the Duchess to see the progress made in the work, with which she seemed much pleased. When still further advanced, the Duke of W. and some of the relatives saw the bust, and all they expressed was very encouraging to me. One day the Duchess brought a gentleman to see the model. As he looked at it, he said that it was too serious a character. "Now, Mr. Gibson," said he, "I should prefer to see the Duchess modelled with that cheerful gay look, as she appears when receiving her friends." Her Grace smiled. I then said that the expression of cheerfulness and gaiety was beneath the dignity of sculpture. When the cast of the bust was completed, the Duchess spoke of it to her Majesty. The Queen and the Prince Consort expressed an anxiety to see it, so the bust was sent to Windsor, and the opinion which they expressed respecting the bust was sent to me to Rome, which afforded me very great pleasure.

The cast of the bust arrived at Rome, and I finished it in marble, and now it is at Apsley House.

CHAPTER XVIII

INCIDENTS FROM ROMAN LIFE—LADY BEAUCHAMP'S VISIT—ETEOCLES AND POLYNICES

I WILL now leave my classical subjects for a few minutes and relate an incident which happened in my neighbourhood, and caused much talk among the Romans.

A woman in low circumstances had a husband who was in the habit, now and then, of coming home intoxicated; often upon such occasions he would ill-treat his poor wife even to beating her. One night he returned home in a worse state than usual, and unable therefore to insult her, he went directly to bed. She soon perceived that he had fallen into a deep sleep. Standing over him watchfully, anxiously, and listening to his snoring, the remembrance of the many beatings she had received from his iron hands rushed like a torrent upon her mind, vengeance quickened her pulsations. The woman meditated, planned, decided. Soon she began her operations, brought forth her instrument of bright steel—womanlike, it was her needle and

thread. It would puzzle the reader to guess what
followed.   Sitting upon a chair close to the bedside
she began to sew the upper and under sheets till he
was entirely closed in, moving her chair as she
advanced with her labour.   The beast was now
secured in his lair, the weaker one, by her artfulness,
had imprisoned the strong ; this being done, feeling
her own security, she glanced her fiery eyes to a
corner of the room, where her husband had several
walking sticks, the weight of some she had often
felt upon her poor back.   She then examined the
sticks and made a choice of one fit for her purpose,
weighty and strong.   Balancing the weapon in her
hand, she felt satisfied that it would answer her
purpose.   Now for vengeance ! Blows after blows
fell unmercifully upon her guilty victim ; his groans
in his perfect helplessness at last brought some of
the neighbours to the spot, the sufferer they could
not see, but saw the sheets of the bed covered with
blood.   The poor woman then sat upon the chair
panting for breath with the fatigue she had gone
through : her husband was not killed, nor did she
intend his death   The next day she was taken off
to prison : during the trial, when the use of the
needle and thread was described, the Judge covered
his face with his hands and shook with laughter
in a most undignified manner; he nevertheless
condemned the woman to a month's imprisonment,
which we all considered extremely severe.

Among my works there is a statue of a lady standing with her hands crossed before her, and a shawl is arranged in folds round about her figure, the head is adorned with ivy, which is gold, as well as her other ornaments, the dress is enriched with a border of red and blue, a slight flesh tint, and blue eyes. It is a portrait of Mrs. Murray, now the Dowager Countess Beauchamp.[1]

This statue I executed for her Ladyship's mother, the Baroness Bray. The Baroness and her most amiable daughters have been to Rome several times, and they became my most kind friends for many years. The statue is placed in the house of the Baroness Bray.

When I was in England Lady Beauchamp requested me to paint her statue, for she had learnt from friends who had seen my coloured Venus at Rome how pleasing the effect was. I complied with her Ladyship's wish, and painted the statue. One day she wrote me a note expressing an anxiety to see me. I waited upon her, and she told me with some uneasiness that not one of the party she had the last evening approved of a coloured statue. I then said, " Lady Beauchamp, do as I do, fight it out with them, it does not signify whether they like it or not." I then invited my friends with her Ladyship's permission to her house, those friends were Sir Charles and Lady Eastlake, Mrs Jameson,

---

[1] I.e , in 1859.

Sir C. Barry and Mr. Cockerell.   Her Ladyship
was also present when they were all standing before
the statue.   The effect soon began to impress them
agreeably, and the longer they dwelled upon the
statue, the more they admired the charm of Polychromy.   I was told that Mr. Cockerell spoke of
the effect of my statue with approbation at a meeting of artists.   I feel with Cicero (in his De
Finibus) that—" the testimony of the multitude is
not of the greatest possible weight, for in every
art, or study, or science, as in Virtue itself, whatever is most excellent, is also most rare."

Artists always lament the ignorance of the
multitude with respect to that art with which they
are most familiar, but I fear that this deficiency of
knowledge in painting and sculpture never can be
much improved, for few will devote a sufficient
portion of their time to the serious attention which
such a difficult subject requires.   More than a little
knowledge is necessary, even to become a tolerable
judge of our art.

Apollonius Tyanaeus says, " That which is best
is always hard to be found out, hard to be judged."
Still, if everyone were equally ignorant of art, if
this were so, how happens it that the most celebrated artists have become known even in their
lifetime, and that they still maintain their eminence ?   We artists after all must confess that there
are a few judges in existence, men who have

devoted a considerable portion of their lives to
the contemplation of their greatest works, who
have read and conversed with the most enlightened
artists.   I say enlightened, because there are many
in the profession who are not so, and still their
mediocre works are purchased, that is, by those
who are ignorant—those whose ignorance they
complain of so much.   Now I think such artists
ought to rejoice in the scarcity of judges, for if
they were very numerous, men of this standard
would starve and the number of such works as
they produce would be greatly diminished.   If
judges are few, nature has been liberal to a great
portion of mankind, for she has bestowed upon them
a delightful gift—a natural taste for the beautiful.

The artist who has the greatest power of affecting the feelings of such will be eulogised, but
that power of touching the feelings of others,
alone, is not sufficient to secure for him lasting
fame; his genius must be accompanied by deep
knowledge of all the higher principles of his art,
and with the power of perfect execution.   Such an
artist must be great, and may hope to live beyond
his time—yes, I fancy that he may say to himself
what Heraclitus said : " If you should return to
life five hundred years hence, you would find
Heraclitus alive, but not the least print of your
names "   The man who has left behind him great
works lives ; those who do not, die and are for-

gotten. That is true which Cicero says, " What is most excellent is also rare."

The remarkable sculptors of our time in Europe are very few, and their best works form a very small number; therefore the inferior are numerous. How rare is genius—the more to be valued. I have always considered indifferent works as valuable to a certain extent; not only do they serve as beacons to show us what to shun; when in juxtaposition with excellence they act as foils, the beautiful appears more beautiful; brighter and brighter still they shine, and will shine for ever. So true is it what Plotinus says in a moral sense, " For the experience of evil produces a clearer knowledge of good."

Again I turn my thoughts to thee, oh Nature! and ever with renewed veneration, for thou art my true teacher. In order that my mind may be more prepared to appreciate and profit by thy dictates, I have endeavoured to remove all false conceptions from my mind, which might have led me from the contemplation of thy immutable laws. Yes, thou art ever beautiful, and clothed in magnificence; but as there is also much of imperfection in Nature, we must be careful to distinguish between the different degrees of the perfect which are presented to our view. It is the duty of the artist to unite into one whole the scattered beauties of Nature: thus by abstraction springs forth ideal beauty.

Thou art ever my guide, oh Nature ! enlighten

my soul, enrich my ideas. I will follow thee, nor will I wander astray with those who forget thee, who violate thy laws, and in consequence sink into oblivion. Yes, it is through thee alone, oh my guide, that I may hope for fame hereafter. Fame, alas! not so lasting as that achieved by thy favoured disciples of ancient Hellas.

Having always been a faithful disciple of Nature, and having imbued myself in the early part of my career with a knowledge of Greek art, I am enabled to profit by all the various beauties which Nature so lavishly offers to my view.

I must here observe that the movements of the multitude in this and in all warm climates are more favourable to art than in countries where Nature is less propitious. All foreign artists and most observing persons are struck with the easy, graceful motions of the common class of Rome, as well as of the peasantry of the neighbourhood, the development of their unrestrained passions being at times so full of expression, so adapted to art. By all these circumstances the inventive faculties of the artist are enriched; then his compositions become more natural and more graceful than that which is purely conventional.

One day on my way to my studio I witnessed in the Via Laurina a scene full of expression. The parties were two young men, seemingly full of rage with each other, and there was between them a young woman who clung to the man who appeared to belong to her; her hand was upon his breast, which was panting with rage; whilst in this action her face was turned to the other with an expression of great excitement All this time the three persons were silent and pale. I could not see a knife in their hands, a rather unusual circumstance in such cases, no people were near, excepting myself. The incident now brought before me led me at once to treat a subject which had been in my mind for a long time, namely, the quarrel between Eteocles and Polynices, on which occasion their mother Jocasta interceded. I began this energetic and grand subject in basso-relievo, and spent a long time over the model.

" *Polynices*   there
              Will I oppose thee front to front, there kill thee.
    Eteocles   . My soul's on fire to meet thee
    Jocasta   . . . wretched me '
          What will you do, my sons?" [1]

I have represented Polynices looking at his brother with calm dignity, and pointing with his sword, as if saying to him, "There will I oppose thee," whilst Eteocles, full of rage and impetuously with his uplifted sword, "My soul's on fire to meet thee."

Jocasta is placed between her sons, and holding Polynices by the left wrist, so as to detain him in order that she may reconcile him to his brother;

[1] Euripides, *Phoenissae*, ll. 623-4.

ETEOCLES AND POLYNICES: JOCASTA INTERVENING.

(From the original drawing.)

at the same time. she turns to Eteocles, putting her hand upon his breast, to check his impetuous rush forward

"Black choler filled his breast that boiled with ire,
And from his eye-balls flashed the living fire "

These lines I repeated often to myself, when modelling the figure of Eteocles. Jocasta is richly attired, with a diadem on her head, and her veil falling back in graceful folds : her whole character is queen-like, and in her tribulation dignified : her soul is harassed by the conduct of Eteocles. I must confess that I am proud of this basso-relievo. Years ago Marshal Marmont visited Rome, and he did me the honour to come to my studio. After shewing him all my works, with which he seemed much pleased, I accompanied him to the small room where my basso-relievo of Eteocles and Polynices was : he looked a considerable time at it, and said, "This is the finest of all your works"; and he continued to dwell upon it. I have never had an order to execute this model in marble, subjects of grandeur and heroic energy seldom attract the notice of the public.

Subjects of beauty and grace are those which attract the most attention, the rich purchase such for then dwellings. I never could approve of obscure subjects for marble, which require the sculptor's own explanation; such are most of the subjects drawn from modern poetry and novels.

Even Milton's Paradise Lost has been found to supply little for the sculptor's art ; and there are but few in the Bible calculated for the decoration of private dwelling-houses   Let me fly rather to the bowers of ancient Hellas : there I enjoy riches in greater abundance, beauty and elevation of character, repose with serenity and dignity ; we have energy also of action, the young hero rushing to the attack ; in one quarter bodily pain supported by dignity, in another, the young virgin resigning up her life for her country—the terrible vengeance of ill-requited affection.   The guilty conscience hunted down by the dreadful Furies.   The sister's love exhibited even at the cost of life ; maternal devotion ; the chastisement of an infamous wife : the guilty punished ; virtue rewarded ; the arrows of divine wrath falling upon the Greek hosts to avenge the outrage committed upon the priest, and all the various vicissitudes of love.   It is in the classic vales that I feel inspired, and my ambition raised higher and higher.   There I see the distant temple where presides the child of golden Hope, as Fame is termed by Sophocles.

Human nature is the same now as it was three thousand years ago.   The sculptor who represents her in all her beauty of form and under all her emotions, will always affect the enlightened mind in all ages, although it may not wholly depend upon the classic names which have been assumed.

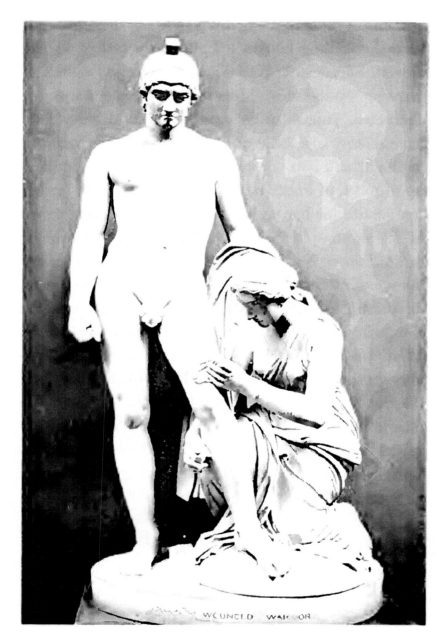

THE WOUNDED WARRIOR.

CHAPTER XIX

GREEK BEAUTY AT ROME—GRAZIA

I BELIEVE Winckelmann says that now and then might be seen at Rome a face equal in beauty to Greek sculpture. We have had such an instance in a girl named Grazia of Capua. Artists of all nations, at Rome, pronounced her the greatest beauty they had ever seen. She was a model only for the head. Here was a living being remarkably close in features to the Greek Ideal—her expression was slightly gloomy. The tragic grandeur of her countenance was most impressive, every part of the features was Greek, her eyes were large and black, the eyebrows black and strong, and where they met drooping a little, which gave an expression of sternness. The form of her mouth with the very short upper lip was perfect; the hair grew low upon the forehead. Her head of black hair in such profusion might have excited envy in any woman.

Grazia treated all the artists with great haughtiness; she had a deficient temper, and it was always difficult to induce her to keep the position which the artist required, for on a cross word being addressed to her she would immediately march out and leave the poor artist to his own operations. My friend Mr. Buckner, now a well-known portrait-painter, was painting her one day; she was sitting in a most provoking attitude, and he, poor man! forgot himself and said something sharp to her. The girl said nothing, but got up from the chair, went to the corner of the room, and took up her shawl over her arm. Returning to him, she looked in his face in silence, then down at his feet, then raising herself up (she was tall), walked majestically away. Mr. B. was much disturbed at this circumstance, believing that she would never sit again to him. The next morning he went to the Corso, and there turned into a jeweller's shop, and purchased a beautiful gold ornament, then called upon the tyrant. He found her at home. Grazia advanced, grave and grand. B. made his bow, and begged her pardon with humility for the scolding which he gave her, at the same time produced the gold ornament, asking her acceptance. She condescended to receive it and all was made up again.

There may be seen in the streets of Rome, during summer, groups of young women and girls dancing and playing upon their tambourines. Grazia one evening gave such a ball, she herself led the dance, playing spiritedly upon her tambourine before her own house; on the opposite side was a large convent with high windows. The next day she received an injunction from the Superior of that establishment not to dance there any more. After some time had elapsed, Grazia felt in the humour to renew her gaieties, and heedlessly invited her party to the same place. That same night, about two in the morning (the hour generally of arresting people), when in deep sleep she was awakened by repeated thundering knocks at her door. She rose, and opened, when the carabinieri said, "La Grazia." They ordered her to dress instantly, and soon she was put into a coach which they had brought; she was then driven at once to prison, and there she was left for several days. After having been set at liberty, Grazia called upon me and related the above occurrence.

As she had money upon her person when in prison, she was allowed to send for any additional food; she did not complain excepting of the bed which was a large sack of straw. Oh, ye worshippers of art and nature, behold the most beautiful girl in Europe in prison sleeping upon straw; she who had been sent for by Royal visitors at Rome to be seen and rewarded by them!

I had often meditated a bust of Grazia, but delayed on account of her insolent and capricious ways. One day Lord Kilmorey encouraged me to begin, saying that he wished her bust in marble. I then engaged the girl to sit to me; she was as usual full of engagements. I wrote my name at the bottom of her long list, and I had to wait three weeks for my turn. At that time, fortunately for me, I had two young lady friends modelling in the room where Grazia was to sit for her bust. One of the ladies was the youngest daughter of the cele-brated Mr. Somerville; the other was Miss Lloyd[1] of Rhagatt, N Wales. She is very clever in painting and modelling animals. Miss Somerville spoke Italian beautifully, and kept Grazia in the best humour possible all the time of the sittings. Grazia believed that every Signora Inglese could speak her language; it was dangerous for any lady to come and look at her and not to say a word to her. I have forgotten to mention a painful incident which happened at the studio of Mr. B., portrait-painter.

Lady —— came in to look at Grazia. Her Ladyship understood Italian, but never said one word to the girl: when she was retiring out of the room, not yet out, Grazia cried out with all her might, "Che brutta vecchia!"[2] Poor B. could not say a word to her for having insulted her Ladyship in his studio.

I took immense pains with the bust, and felt happy to model such an extraordinary beauty. There came one day a lady anxious to see Grazia,

---

[1] Miss Lloyd was a pupil of Gibson's
[2] "What an ugly old frump!"

but did not understand Italian, and she stared at
the girl very steadfastly in silence. Turning to me,
she said, with a feeling of disappointment, " Is *this*
the beauty ? " I had already observed a gathering
cloud over the girl's black brows ; her eyes began
to kindle. The lady then said to me, "And what
an atrocious expression she has ! " Grazia darted
her fiery looks at me, and said in an inquisitive,
sarcastic tone, " Cosa dice la Signora ? " [1] Instantly
I said, " Dice che siete molto bella." [2] She was
then greatly pleased and flattered, and a tinge of
red came into her cheeks, which gave a charm to
her dark brown complexion ; and thus, by a great
deviation from truth, I saved this lady from some
gross and insulting expression My mother would
have grieved over this infringement upon truth,
for, as I have related, she once flogged me well for
a lie and theft.

Another day Lady Davy came to pay a visit to
our savage beauty I warned her ladyship as to
her deportment to Grazia when in her presence.
Lady Davy spoke Italian incorrectly, although
with fluency, so the moment my lady entered the
room she addressed herself most kindly to the girl,
and began to compliment her upon her great
beauty, saying, " Bellissima davvero," [3] and, after
chattering some time, took her leave. Grazia then,

[1] " What did the lady say ? " [2] She says you are very beautiful."
[3] " Very beautiful, indeed "

with a downcast look, said in a low tone to herself,
" Che cara Signora spero che tornerà." [1]   I finished
the model of the bust, and executed it for Lord
Kilmorey.   Afterwards I executed a repetition for
Queen Victoria, and on the front of the bust is
inscribed

GRAZIA.

FILIA CAPUENSIS.

When Mrs. Huskisson was at Rome she was a
great admirer of our celebrated beauty.   At that
time there was a German who gave *tableaux
vivants* at the Theatro Valle ; the most beautiful
of the models were selected.   Grazia was shown
off to great advantage, dressed up from Raphael's
Muse of Poetry, with a lyre in her hand, and
crowned with laurel.   When the curtain was withdrawn the applause was thundering, again and
again, and repeated cries of " Ancora ! "   Mrs.
Huskisson said that it was the most beautiful sight
she ever saw in her life.

Among the vulgar at Rome Grazia's moral
character was vilified.   A Roman painter, young
and very handsome, and a friend of mine, confessed to me that he had set his heart upon putting
her virtue to the test, and he engaged her to sit to
him.   Upon this occasion he declared his love, and
his offers were liberal, for he had tolerable means
at his disposal.   She got up from the chair, and

---

[1] " The dear lady, I hope she will come again "

said, " Is it for this I am sent for ?   No, I despise
you and your money." and then walked out of the
room, and would never return.

The plebeian class here are very fond of wearing
gold and silver ornaments even to profusion, but
our Grazia had no such ambition, though she could
well afford it.   As Athenaeus quotes :

"Carmus the Syracusan said, Beauty unadorn'd adorn'd the most."

When Grazia was about twenty-five she married
a baker, and had a child, after whose birth she
never recovered her strength ; the doctors advised
her to go to her native air, Capua ; thither she
went, and soon died.

Among those who painted numerous portraits of
Grazia, we had here at that period a young noble-
man of talent. the Earl of Compton, who produced
some pictures which did his Lordship much credit.
His best work was " The Judgment of Paris," a performance deserving of great praise, which was
justly given to it.   He drew and painted many
portraits of Grazia.   If she had been born at
Athens in the days of Phidias I feel certain that
she would have been modelled by him and his
pupils ; for she was so very near to that ideal
beauty which the Greeks produced in their sculpture,
and I have no doubt whatever that she would have
gained the prize at the contests of beauty which
were established among those wonderful and most

refined people of Greece. Both young men and women entered into these contests.

Theophrastus says, that "there is also a contest of beauty which takes place among the Eleans, and that the decision is come to with great care and deliberation," and he adds, " In some places there are contests between the women in respect to modesty and good management." With respect to beauty he adds, " This is the gift of chance or of nature ; but that the honour paid to modesty ought to be one of greater degree. For that it is in consequence of modesty that beauty is beautiful ; for, without modesty, it is apt to be subdued by intemperance."

Socrates said, " Outward beauty was a sign of inward beauty, and therefore chose such auditors.' " In the Life of Man, as in an Image, every part ought to be beautiful," and he used to recommend young men to be constantly looking in the glass, in order that, if they were handsome, they might be worthy of their beauty ; and if they were ugly, they might conceal their unsightly appearance by their accomplishments.

Victoria of Albano was a great beauty, and very Greek. She would not sit to artists, but consented to be painted by the celebrated Chevalier Vernet. So her beauty will not be preserved for future ages by the sculptor, with his more lasting material.

LUISA—A WOMAN OF
THE SABINES.

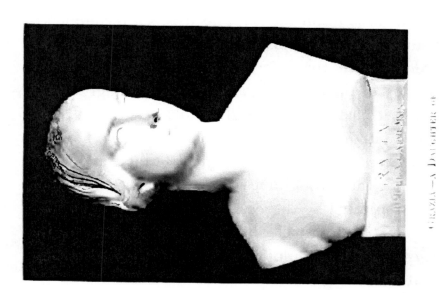

GRAZIA—A DAUGHTER OF
CAPUA.

I will also mention a third fair one—her name was Assunta; she was painted by many, and by Chevalier Riedel for Queen Victoria. He also painted for H.M. one of the dark Arab-looking girls; the Queen was greatly pleased with these two beautiful paintings.

CHAPTER XX

DIONYSOS

In the year 1856, Lord Londonderry returned to
Rome, and often visited my studio with her Ladyship. His Lordship was one of the many who did
not approve of colouring my statues, but he was
desirous to possess some work by me. So he decided, and proposed that the subject should be a
youthful male beauty of the first class. A God—
Bacchus. "That will do, Per Bacco," said I—yes,
I will undertake such a subject with delight It
is improper to represent him according to the
ideas of the masses of people, in a state of
inebriation.

I have represented Dionysos, the Son of Jove,
standing, with a god-like dignity and youthful
grace, having his sceptre (the Thyrsus) in his left
hand, and in the right his cup of wine. The God
is not going to drink it, but to bestow the gift.
His head is richly adorned with ivy, and as he is
the "lover of flowers" there are flowers mixed in

his wreath, a fillet twines round his brow, and falls with his locks on each side of the neck.

"The gold-haired Dionysos"

The expression of his divine countenance is that of tranquillity and sweetness, the upper and lower eyelids are a little swelled, which gives softness and a slight touch of dreamy voluptuousness to his feminine countenance, whilst his lips are a little apart, "as if a word was hovering there." His form is purely abstract, therefore refined to the utmost.

Besides the male models I employed a female one also, so as to enter thoroughly into the spirit of the Greek idea, that Apollo, Dionysos and Eros are androgynous.

I have introduced a lyre at his feet, " The Muse-leader," "dance-rouser"; for giving Bacchus a lyre, I was called to account by three English gentlemen of high education, saying that there were no statues of that God represented with that instrument. I confessed that I had never seen such a thing, but still I had my authority, for Calistratus describes a bronze figure of Bacchus by Praxiteles with a lyre, and that bronze was coloured. People say truly, we have done with the Gods, nor do we concern ourselves about them any more; those subjects do not interest or touch our feelings; but I say we sculptors have to do with those Gods in marble, for they teach us all that is beautiful and sublime in our art. Those persons are influenced by their religious feelings: nor have they any pleasure in high art. It is beauty and perfection of the human form that the sculptor must labour for. It is in the Vatican he will be enlightened. If we had never seen Greek art, we sculptors would have been mere imitators of Nature as we find her; there are many who advocate literal copying of Nature as we find her, but I want my soul to rise above the common multitude—yes, my soul flies after the beautiful.

Proclus says, " He who takes for his model such forms as Nature produces, and confines himself to an exact imitation of them, will never attain to what is perfectly beautiful, for the works of Nature are full of disproportion, and fall very short of the true standard of beauty." This is a fact which concerns the sculptor of high ambition. I have no doubt Proclus repeats the above principle of selection from the writings of the Greek artists.

With respect to my Bacchus, my cast-off heathen God—the fact is that the human mind feels an inward pleasure in the contemplation of the beautiful human form with its appropriate expression under any denomination whatever. This being the fact, I watched the impression made upon the feelings of the numerous persons who came to see my clay model of the youthful God.

I, the sculptor, will venture to confess that their sentiments were unanimously pleasing to myself. Quintilian says so truly, " The learned understand the reason of art, the unlearned feel the pleasure."

After Lord Londonderry ordered the statue of Bacchus, he came to the studio, took his leave of me, and left Rome for England ; but when he was about to start from the door, his lordship turned round and said, " Now, don't you go and paint my statue." I made no reply.

The following winter, when modelling the Bacchus, Lord and Lady Portarlington came to Rome. One evening I went to a large party, bowed to the lady of the house, and soon observed Lady Portarlington sitting on a sofa. I went up to her and made my bow. " Oh, I wanted to see you," said her ladyship. " Is it true that you have said to some persons that you will paint my brother's statue of Bacchus ? " " Yes," I said, " it is true." Then she said sharply, " But my brother told you not to paint his statue." " He did so, but I am determined to colour it." She appeared angry and silent, when a gentleman, fortunately for me, came up, and addressed himself to her. I then stole away to another quarter of the room.

When Lord and Lady Londonderry again returned to Rome in the year 1859 they soon came to see the model of Bacchus   It seems many persons who had seen it in clay gave them a flattering

account of it.   They were greatly pleased and often
returned to contemplate it.   I began to introduce
the subject of Polychromy, saying that it would give
great charm to the effect of the statue.   His
Lordship said, "Can it be removed afterwards?"
I said, "You had better not try."   He then turned
to her Ladyship and said, "Now you see, if you
want a work by this man, you must take it as he
chooses to turn it out, or not have it at all!"   "I am
certain," said I, "that when this statue is seen in
England, adorned with classic elegance, it will be
run down, but that will be no proof that I am in
the wrong.   I contend boldly for the colouring, the
effect of which I greatly admire, but I venture no
opinion as to the merits of my work.   I leave this
to be decided by judges."   The fact is I never have
been able to satisfy myself yet with any one work
which I have produced, for in my imagination there
is a degree of beauty which I am unable to reach.
On the front of the plinth of my Bacchus is the
following :

Ο ΔΙΟΣ ΠΑΙΣ ΔΙΟΝΥΣΟΣ

I will now enter upon a subject of interest—a
subject which requires great judgment, knowledge,
and imagination.   It is a national monument to the
Duke of Wellington.   The following ideas were
the result of my meditations.

The design for a monument to His Grace the Duke of Wellington, appropriate to a Place of Worship.

The base of the Tomb is a parallelogram, upon which is an octagonal Pedestal, supporting a sarcophagus, upon which is the figure of the Duke. All the subjects represented upon the Tomb are intended to illustrate one great and sublime moral— that all human greatness must terminate in death, and that at the sound of the last trumpet, the dead shall rise again to eternal life,

Description of the subjects.

The Duke is represented lying in death, enveloped in his mantle and with his sword.

Bassi-relievi.

Upon the upper part of the Tomb are all the victories of the warrior assembled together; they are led on by Fame, in procession, chanting to the glory of their Hero.

Upon the base is the return of Peace in triumph, amidst a rejoicing people. Victory brings Peace back in her own chariot drawn by four horses, and she is followed by Plenty, Science, Commerce, and Agriculture: the latter turns round and offers her pruning-hook to a soldier who is in the act of breaking his lance. An old veteran meets his

daughter.   On the other side of the Tomb is the
door, having on the one side Faith, and on the other
Hope.   Upon the two ends of the Tomb are
medallions of the Duke at two periods of his life.

The Statues.

Returning to the front, on the right of the Tomb,
is Military Glory, bearing the British standard
crowned with laurel ; on the left stands History,
meditating upon the exploits of the hero.   From
History we come to the Angel of Death, with the
reverted torch in his hand, and he is crowned with
poppies.   From Death we come to the Angel of
Life.   " The Angel of the Lord," waiting intently
for the divine signal from above, when, by the
blast of his trumpet, slumbering generations shall
wake to life eternal.

" A Ω "

When I was in England, I submitted the above
ideas in words to a friend whom I consider the
best judge in the country, a man of highly cultivated mind   After meditating a little upon the
subject, he said, " It's a grand conception."   When
I returned to Rome, I put my thoughts, as written
above, into plastic form, and my model met with
the approbation of the best native judges here.   I
sent it to the competition, but its great simplicity,
among the numerous florid, confused, and ignorant

abuses of allegory, attracted no notice from those gentlemen who were appointed as judges.

My friend, whose judgment I think so highly of, and is considered such by the high in station there, decided not to give any opinion upon any one of the models there. I believe it was from the fear of bringing himself under the vengeance of those papers in the interests of the artists in London. When I saw that curious collection, I soon perceived that not one of the celebrated sculptors of Europe had sent any design ; but when I observed my own model there, I liked it more than ever.

The custom which prevails among the Roman sculptors of visiting each other's studios, and making critical remarks on the clay models which they are engaged upon, has a most salutary effect, which is felt by all of them. During the progress of my own clay models, I always encourage criticism from the artists who visit my studio, and when I go to them, they expect me to point out any defects in their works which may strike me.

I believe the painters in the same way invite observations on the cartoons upon which they are engaged.

A great many years ago the celebrated German painter, Cornelius, Thorwaldsen the sculptor, and some three or four scholars were invited by a young Saxon of the name of Plattner to give their opinion respecting a cartoon on which he had been working for a considerable time.   Plattner was not a genius, but a very amiable man, and much esteemed by all.

Behold the great cartoon, Cornelius, Thorwaldsen, and Plattner standing before it, all in dead silence, Plattner awaiting anxiously to hear the judgment which he expected to be pronounced upon his work. After some time had elapsed in profound silence, Cornelius in deep thought, in an instant, without uttering a word, ran up to the cartoon, and jumped smack through the middle of it.   Thorwaldsen seeing this, also ran on and jumped after Cornelius, right through ; then the scholars, like so many hounds, leaped one after the other, and followed their leader.   Poor Plattner, what did he do ?   He also followed the rest, and through he flew, and joined the laughter of the whole company.

It seems that the composition of the cartoon was very defective, for the artist had divided his design into two equal parts, leaving the centre empty, and it was through the vacant space that the stern, severe judges took their leap.   However, this terrible affair had its beneficial effect ; for it cured the poor artist from his useless ambition in pursuit of high art.   Soon after, the post of diplomatic agent was given to him.

CHAPTER XXI

HIS LAST WORKS—THE ROYAL VISITS TO ROME—THE
KING OF BAVARIA'S TRIBUTE TO HIS HONOUR—THE
LAST VISIT TO ENGLAND—HIS LAST DAYS

MANY persons have said that I should model the
design of Christ blessing the children, but I think
it would be out of place among classical statues.
I had another very good subject, it was Minerva;
after taming Pegasus, she brings him to Belle-
rophon, that he may mount him to go and attack
the Chimera. I have never seen this beautiful
subject treated by any sculptor. Saulini has made
a fine cameo from my small model of it. " Christ
blessing the Children " would do in a room by itself.
I have also finished a model of a small monument
to Mrs. Huskisson. There arose a coolness between
me and the Clergy of the Cathedral of Chichester
owing to this sculpture. I refused to comply with
their request to send a design for their approval
and refused to pay for the place. They also wanted
to see the inscription, which I also refused. It
seemed the affair got about and some ladies, friends
of Mrs. Huskisson, said that they were throwing

obstacles in the way of her monument. They gave in and I am not to pay anything for the place.

I spent most of the winter of 1859 modelling a group representing what I saw in the street, a few years ago, when I made a sketch of the action— a girl of about fourteen throwing up a child and kissing it. This clay model occupied me for three months. It was ordered last year by Mr. Matcham, a Scotch gentleman, also a repetition for Mr. W. R. Sandbach.

I saw much of the Prince of Wales[1] during his visit to Rome. I took him to forty studios, the Vatican, the Capitol, Villa Albani If H.R.H. had prolonged his stay here I should have taken him to forty more studios. He was not allowed to order anything, but he broke through that prohibition when he saw my pupil Miss Hosmer, and on the morning of his departure ordered her little statue of Puck. Colonel Bruce, his equerry, told me it was altogether his own act. On the same morning, he said in a low voice, " Follow me," and bolted into the garden. There he presented me with a splendid diamond ring. I found afterwards that he had presented one to Mr. Pentland, who accompanied him to see the ancient remains here. The young Prince made a favourable impression upon all here. He gave me

[1] The late King Edward VII

his portrait in a photograph The ring I will display now and then for his sake.

I also modelled the bust of Prince Duleep Singh. His Highness left more than a week ago for England. He always went to parties here in his native dress, and so I modelled his bust, which he ordered in marble

I must now write of the honour that I have received, the greatest honour that can be bestowed upon an artist and that from a foreign Sovereign. King Louis of Bavaria has placed a marble statue of me in a niche in the Glyptothek, next to one of Tenerani, one of Thorwaldsen, and of Routh. These statues, I am told, stand in niches outside the building. His Majesty is going to adorn the other side of the building with statues of ancient sculptors. The King sent me a message of kind remembrance and that he had placed the statue of me in its place. I wrote a letter of thanks to be laid before His Majesty. This is a copy :—

" ROME,
" *May 6th*, 1859 "

" MY DEAR SIR,

" Since you kindly delivered to me the gracious message from His Majesty Louis King of Bavaria, I venture to express through you my grateful sentiments which I beg may be forwarded, and I hope laid before his Majesty with my humble duty.

Q

" It is difficult for me to find words sufficient to convey the deep sense of gratitude which I feel by so great an honour as that of a statue of myself ordered by His Majesty and placed by the side of one of Thorwaldsen, Tenerani, and Routh at the Glyptothek.

" The kindness which I have received for so many years from His Majesty during his visits to Rome had already left upon my mind a lasting impression of his benevolence, but now he has been pleased to confer a distinction upon me greater than anything which I could have presumed to imagine. I am proud of this honour, as it has been conferred upon me by the greatest patron of art since ancient times, and by a Sovereign who has formed the purest school of high art since its decline. The noble works of those great men whom he has raised will certainly go down to posterity with the immortal name of their enlightened and Royal Patron.

" Permit me, my dear Sir, to offer you my thanks for your kind participation upon this occasion, and believe me always,

" Yours sincerely,

" JOHN GIBSON."

" To Professor Schoepf."

I wished to present a copy of my book to His Majesty King Louis. He did not accept, and the following letter was sent in reply :—

HEBE.

(ΗΒΗ ΘΕΩΝ ΚΑΛΛΙΣΤΑ)

"M. le Baron de Cetts, it is against my custom to accept of any presents, and I desire you will say so to Mr. Gibson, with my most friendly thanks for his attention in contemplating sending me a copy of his work

"He knows how highly I esteem him A full length statue has, for some time, been placed in one of the outside niches of my Glyptothek.

"With sentiments of much esteem,

"Your well intended,

"S S. LUDWIG."

"BERCHLESGADEN,

   "*July* 23*rd*, 1861."

During the winter of 1860 I was much employed in modelling a figure of Hebe. The commission was given me nearly three years ago by Mr. Howard Galton, who ordered me to colour it; which I did with great pleasure. I also finished my Pandora, and as she was ordered to be coloured. she now appeared in all her splendour. Some persons have said that my Hebe is the best female statue I have modelled. I must confess that I had pleased myself with this Goddess of Youth She is about sixteen "Hebe, ever fair and ever young."

Miss Hosmer modelled a child subject which no one has done. It is the dead body of Astyanax laid out upon his father's shield. His head is adorned with the funeral crown; a band is tied

under his chin to keep his mouth closed ; flowers
are scattered about him, all according to the custom
relating to the dead.   The little Prince looks
beautiful in death, and the story is affecting.
Round the edge of the shield you read in Greek,
" Astyanax, Son of Hector."   I also modelled a
group of a young warrior wounded and a woman
medicating his wound.   It is the sign of life.   A
clever German sculptor said of this to me, " You
had better leave that group behind you in marble
than leave money."

The summer of 1861 was spent in England.
Gibson states he " got so involved in London with
engagements in town and out of town " that he
could not go to Liverpool or to Hafod-un-nos, as
he intended.   Still he found time to model a bust of
Sir Charles Lyell, and at his own request a medallion
of Lady Mary C. Stanhope.   Early the following
winter he was back at Rome and gave his time to
modelling the basso-relievo " Christ blessing the
Children."   This was a great attraction ; numbers
of people visited the studio every day to see it.   It
made a great impression, the head of Christ impressed
them more than Gibson hoped, particularly the
ladies ; some of them said, " The head of our Lord,"
in a low tone of reverence, a circumstance which
must have given him the liveliest satisfaction, for
he had a hesitation, natural to a deeply religious

CHRIST BLESSING THE CHILDREN.

(To face p. 292.)

man, concerning the head of Christ "The fear of failing came over me," he says "I had to express the Divine from within perceived through outward form—the form of man—elevated, beautiful, and benevolent"

However, he was interrupted in his desire to finish this. "The most beautiful lady I have ever seen has been here, for a short time only—she was the cause of taking me from the · Christ blessing the Children' for twenty-five days. It was Lady Clifden—newly married Lord Clifden came to me and said, 'I am told you decline busts' I said, 'I do.' He expressed the greatest desire that I should undertake his Lady's bust. When I saw her—by Jove, I was surprised when I saw such a Greek face. I said, 'I shall model your Ladyship with delight' Then his Lordship thanked me very much I told her that if she lived in the time of the Greeks she would have gained the prize of beauty I do not expect to see such another, nor one more amiable."

Early in June Miss Hosmer and Gibson set out for England. They had accepted invitations to stay with Lady Eastlake and Lady Marian Alford for the Great Exhibition of 1862. Miss Hosmer's Zenobia and three of Gibson's tinted statues were exhibited—Mrs. Preston's famous tinted Venus— the difficulties in reference to the conditions of the loan being finally overcome; Lady Marian Alford

lent " Pandora," and Mr. Holford "Cupid tormenting the Soul." The well-known architect, Owen
Jones, had constructed a beautiful Greek temple,
simple, chaste, in consonance with the statuary
and to set them off. This was the first time tinted
statuary were exhibited in England, and Gibson's
Polychromy raised a storm of controversy, with a
consensus of opinion generally unfavourable to
tinting, but that did not affect Gibson at all. He
held that " the objections which the majority of
our people have to coloured statues arises not from
real taste and judgment; they are under the influence of custom. They have always seen statues
white, and there they stupidly stick. The statue
must be coloured with delicacy and taste—a conventional effect—not that of a living being. So
done it has a new charm, but the beholder must
have feeling for the beautiful to enjoy it. As for
our home sculptors, one delivers a lecture against
colouring sculpture ; another writes in the papers.
These men are unknown to fame, and no
authority."

"On the 12th November, 1862, the Prince of
Wales, the Prince and Princess of Prussia (the
late Emperor and Empress Frederick of Germany),
arrived at Rome by rail from Civita Vecchia. At
eleven o'clock next morning they were all in the
studio, and the Princess Royal kept them in the
rooms for at least an hour, for she looked at every-

Mr. and Mrs. Preston.   John Gibson.

THE TINTED VENUS AT THE GREAT EXHIBITION OF 1862.

thing, even the casts from Nature—hands, legs,
arms.   She greatly admired the effect of colouring
the statues : that of the ' Girl and Cupid ' for the
Prince of Wales (the late King Edward VII.) was
coloured, as was a small copy of the tinted Venus.
When retiring, the Prince of Prussia invited me
to dine the same evening, and a very happy evening I passed.   Her Royal Highness spoke to me
much, and said she greatly admired tinting the
statues.   After a few days came another invitation
to dine with the Prince of Prussia, and so I found
myself again in the midst of them all.   After
dinner I was again delighted with our Princess ;
she was so natural and pleasing.   She spoke to
me of the Princess Alexandra (now the Queen
Mother) and considers her very pretty."   The
result was a promise to visit England next summer
to make a portrait bust of the Princess of Wales.

The French still held Rome, and though there
were frequent demonstrations, " that is " Gibson
says, " shouts," the city was perfectly quiet.   It was,
however, so infested with robbers that Gibson expected to be attacked every night.   He escaped
assault   Penry Williams, however, was not so
fortunate, for he was attacked and robbed of his
gold watch and was very roughly handled one
night on his way up the stairs to dine with some
friends who lived on the Corso.

In accordance with his promise, Gibson came to

England in the summer of 1863. He greatly
appreciated the honour, and writes on keeping
the appointment at Marlborough House—" Well,
here you are ; you have fulfilled your promise," said
the Prince, giving me his hand on my first appearance. " I will go and bring the Princess to you."
He brought his bride. I bowed low—rose my
head. She smiled sweetly. At once I saw what
a pretty subject she was for a bust. I said so, the
Prince smiled.

I modelled the bust at Marlborough House, and
it was done in fourteen days. The Princess sat
eight times—an hour each sitting. She was always
good-natured, full of good sense, and the girlish
playfulness was pretty. The Prince was very much
pleased with my model, and one day he brought his
sister, the Princess Helena, who said it was very like.

When the clay bust was finished, I received the
commands of the Queen to come to Osborne
next day. I arrived there at four o'clock in the
afternoon. The next day at eleven o'clock the
Honourable Mrs. Bruce conducted me to the Queen.
I bowed low, stepped up and said that I felt very
grateful to Her Majesty for this honour—this great
pleasure of seeing Her Majesty. " How long is it
since you were here ? " said the Queen. I replied
that I modelled her bust there in 1850. Thus it
was thirteen years since I had seen her. I was surprised to find how little she had changed ; and as

HER MAJESTY QUEEN ALEXANDRA
(then Princess of Wales)

she conversed on, how cheerful, and often laughing at what I said. She accompanied me through rooms full of statues and pictures—modern works executed at Rome by Italians, Germans, and three Englishmen, including myself. At the close of the interview the Queen said to me, " I will show you my own rooms to-morrow," and this prolonged my stay to two days.

The second day I was again conducted to her Majesty. The Honourable Mrs. Bruce was there The Queen showed me all the works of art in her own sitting room. She was very cheerful. After some time had passed on, Mrs. Bruce said, " Mr. Gibson, what age were you when you first went to Rome?" I could see the Queen was expecting my reply, when I said, " Oh ! Mrs. Bruce, if I were to tell you that you would find out my age." The Queen laughed, and I said, " I will not tell my age to any lady." Her Majesty laughed much. " No," said I, " I have nothing to do with age It is true my beard has become white, much to my annoyance." And I put my hand to my beard. Then Her Majesty laughed again. But I would not tell my age.

When this pleasing interview was over, the Prince of Wales sent for me to walk with him in the grounds. With him were the Princess of Wales and the Princess Louise. Walking with them through the flower gardens Her Royal

Highness gave me a rose. I placed it in my button-
hole, but soon took it out and kept it in my hand.
Soon the Princess said, " Mr. Gibson, where is the
rose ? " I held it out in my left hand and said " the
stem's too short ; it will drop out " Instantly the
Princess Louise said, " Here is one with a longer
stem." I placed both gifts in my breast, next to
my heart, where they will ever bloom. Since I
have arrived here I have been full of engagements.
Invitations to the country I have declined "

Gibson returned to Rome in the autumn, he
worked on, " ever with fresh pleasure." People
amused him often by asking " We suppose you
will soon retire." They thought his object was to
make money, and his reply always was " Have you
ever heard of a poet retiring from writing poetry ?
Sculpture is my poetry." His new subject was a
variation of the story of Psyche, who arrives before
the palace of Pluto. She sees the dog Cerebus, is
startled and stares with wide open eyes at the
monster. She is agitated, her nostrils are dilated—
there is a quivering of the lips : she keeps up her
courage, and her hope of safety is in the cake which
she is about to throw to the three-headed dog.
Whilst Cerebus is eating the cake, Psyche passes
on her journey into the Palace.

The high opinion which Queen Victoria had of
Gibson again found expression on the occasion of
the Memorial to the Prince Consort. The sculptor

himself held Prince Albert in the highest estimation. It was natural, therefore, that the Queen would desire to consult him, and the present memorial, to some extent, follows his suggestions. The final design was again submitted to him for his opinion, and concerning it he states:—"The Memorial to the memory of the Prince Consort is to have four groups in sculpture at the base of the Monument to represent the four quarters of the globe. The Queen made known her pleasure, that she offered me one of the Groups.

It was Europe—each group was to consist of five figures and an animal, to be in bronze or marble. I declined this splendid offer because I considered it would be necessary to me to be in England some part of the time. I could not venture to be in the cold climate of England, after being roasted here for forty-six years. In reply I received the following : "Her Majesty regrets that you cannot undertake the group of Europe—she would so much have liked that your genius should have helped to immortalise the memory of her beloved Prince. But her Majesty quite understands your reasons for declining and your dislike to change the Roman climate for one so cold and unpleasant as our own."

I wrote again, and offered to make the model here at Rome, send it, and that the Queen might have it cast in bronze, or executed in marble by a sculptor in England. Here is the reply: " The Queen was much pleased with your letter, and is so sorry that the plan you suggest had not occurred to you before. Unfortunately, as soon as your refusal to execute the group of Europe was known, it was offered to another sculptor, in order that no time be lost about the Memorial." If I were to stay in England during the cold weather, I should very soon have my throat attacked, for even here in winter I have a tendency that way.

The groups should, however, have no more than three figures; five is a mass of confusion—a rich crowd to attract the admiration of the masses at the expense of simplicity. The following is part of the letter written by Mr. Scott, and sent to me: " Europe is represented by Europa on the Bull, surrounded by representations of the leading nations and races, as England and Germany for the Teutonic races, and Italy and France for those of Latin origin " The architect gives his ideas for the other groups also. In my letter to be laid before the Queen, I ventured to give my own idea how Europe should be represented on a group. Here it is: " Europe stands majestical, crowned, and in her hand is the sceptre, the emblem of government; in the other hand is the Bible, in-dicative of the Christian Church which she pro-pagates. Commerce is represented; also the figure of the Arts. There are two figures in deep meditation: one is Astronomy, looking up at the heavens, the other is Philosophy, with Plato in her hand. Thus the group of five figures represents Europe as the enlightened Nurse of Government, Religion, Commerce, Arts, Astronomy, and Philosophy." In reply I received the following: " The Queen is much struck with your idea of what the group of Europe should be, and thinks it a great improvement on the original plan Her Majesty quite agrees with you that the figure of Jupiter (in the form of a bull) carrying off Europa is not one that should be placed under the Cross, and is much obliged to you for pointing out the incongruity of the conjunction." At any rate, I feel I have done a little service with my pen, if I declined to work with my chisel.

That summer, he did not follow his usual custom of going to the Tyrol, or England. Penry Williams and he had set out for Switzerland but remained at Leghorn, probably, worn out by the fatigue of travelling during the hot season, he felt he did not have the energy to go further. During the following winter he completed his low-relief " Christ blessing the Children." Probably he had given more care to the execution of this than any other work, except, perhaps, the tinted Venus. But age was gradually sapping his strength: his stay at Leghorn the previous summer had certainly not braced him for the winter. The spring of 1865 saw him weaker.

One morning he went out as usual to breakfast at the Greek Caffe, suddenly he fainted—" I opened my eyes," he writes, " and saw persons round me I said to them 'Has anything been the matter with me?' I was taken home in a cab and felt ill. The next day I felt better and went to the studio. There I sat on a chair in my room. I opened my eyes, found myself lying on the floor—drops of blood round me—having wounded my head against the modelling stool. I sent for the Doctor, a German. He was the Physician to the Grand Duke of Tuscany and lived under me. He cured me, but he says, sounding my ribs, that the liver is slightly affected. As I am going to Switzerland, he mentioned a place celebrated for mineral water : I shall go there.

On the 12th of July, 1865, Penry Williams and Gibson set out for their last holiday together. They stayed a week at Leghorn with their dying friend Spence. They spent some time at Lucerne, and as the summer was a cold one, came down to Lake Maggiore There they spent some time, returning slowly to Rome through Milan. He felt very well, and early in October commenced working on with his usual energy and interest He was full of the idea of his last work " Theseus and the Robber.' His pupil, Miss Lloyd, was also back in his studio. He was apparently in good health. but, suddenly, on the 9th of January, he was struck down by paralysis. Subsequent attacks deprived him of speech. Miss Lloyd and Penry Williams were with him to the end, and early on the morning of the 27th of the same month he passed "into the land of cloudless splendour.'

Shortly before his death his last honour was conferred upon him, the Prussian Order of Full Merit. The previous year he had been elected a member of the Academy of Urbino, referring to this, he wrote: " I am now a member of eleven Academies, also of the Legion of Honour—I am a Welshman." It was also characteristic of the man that, following the example of Canova and Thorwaldsen, he bequeathed his models and statues in the studio and his entire fortune to the Royal Academy. For, without presumption, he thought that if they were exhibited in a Gallery, his works might have an influence for good upon future students.

As John Gibson was a member of the Legion of Honour, the General Montebello, commanding the French troops occupying Rome, accorded him military honours A lieutenant's guard formed part of the funeral procession and fired the usual volleys over the grave. Troops also, at the salute with reversed arms, lined the path from the cemetary chapel to the grave, while the muffled drums of the French troops beat their dirge for the great sculptor. Lord Northesk; Chevalier Schnetz;

Director of the French Academy; Chevalier Wolff,
the Prussian sculptor; Chevalier Bravo, the Consul
for Denmark and Sweden, and a well-known artist;
Signor Saulini, the cameo engraver; M. d'Elpinet,
the French sculptor; and two British artists—
Mr. T. Dessoulavy and Mr. T. Colman were the
pall-bearers. The chief mourners were Mr. Odo
Russell, Mr. Severn, the British Consul, and his
best friend, Penry Williams. The service was
conducted by the Rev. Mr. Watts, and would have
had a more public character but for the fear of
offending the Roman government. But the bare-
headed crowds of all nations which lined the streets
testified to the universal respect which he had won
from all. Still, one cannot help thinking the man,
whose character, to quote Lord Lytton's words,
" was in unison with his attributes as an artist,
beautiful in its simplicity and truthfulness. noble in
its dignity and elevation," though he would keenly
have appreciated the honour which the French
people gave him, would still more prefer that the
language of his poetry—the allegory of his
sculpture—were better known, and therefore better
appreciated, by future generations.

APPENDICES

APPENDIX I

CATALOGUE RAISONNÉE OF THE WORKS OF JOHN GIBSON, R.A.[1]

Unpublished Drawings

Subject	Notes and Present Location.
The Fallen Angels . . .	Royal Institution, Liverpool
Drawings to illustrate Dante	
Sketches and Studies . .	Royal Academy.
Sketches and Designs.	

Statuary.

Head of Bacchus .	A copy from a model
Psyche	Exhibited at the first Liverpool Academy.
The Pugilist	His first attempt in Canova's studio —a copy of the statue by Canova at the Vatican At Hafod-un-nos, Denbighshire
Mars and Cupid . . .	His first commission at Rome Chatsworth
The Sleeping Shepherd . .	Walker Art Gallery (Modelled this year.) Exhibited R A, 1835.
Psyche borne aloft by the Zephyrs	The original was made for Sir George Beaumont The replica made for Prince Torlonia is now at the Palazzo Corsini, Rome Another replica at Petersburg

[1] The order is, approximately, chronological

Subject	Notes and Present Location
The Three Graces	This must have been made before Canova's death, as the same group was also executed by both Canova and Thorwaldsen Walker Art Gallery
Paris	Modelled in 1819 Exhibited R A , 1830
Sleeping Shepherd, Boy	Two replicas were made, one of which is at the Walker Art Gallery, Liverpool
Hylas surprised by the Na-iades	Tate Gallery, London Exhibited R A , 1837
Cupid drawing Bow	Wynnstay, N Wales
Nymph preparing for the Bath	Executed for Lord Yarborough Exhibited R A., 1831.
Nymph reposing	Bavaria
Psyche	Exhibited R A , 1827
Venus kissing Cupid . . .	Exhibited R A , 1833.
Cupid disguised as a Shep-herd.	Eight repetitions executed Exhibited R.A., 1837 A repetition at the Walker Art Gallery.
Love tormenting the Soul	Two replicas were made This statue marks an epoch in Gibson's career, for when he was engaged on the model, the idea came to him to tint his statues The replica at Dorchester House is tinted Exhibited R.A , 1839
Venus Verticordia	Exhibited R A , 1839
Proserpine in the Fields of Enna	
Narcissus	Exhibited R A., 1838 Three replicas—one of which at R A
Hunter and the Dog .	Hafod-un-nos Three replicas were made
Eos	Exhibited R A , 1848 Hafod-un-nos One repetition.
Jocasta	Exhibited R A , 1840.
Sappho	Liverpool.
Flora	Two repetitions
Wounded Amazon . .	Eaton Hall One repetition.
Queen Victoria between Jus-tice and Clemency.	Princes Chambers, Westminster.
Venus and Cupid	Marlborough House. Two replicas

Subject.	Notes and Present Location.
The Tinted Venus . . .	Four repetitions were made, one of which, on a smaller scale, is at Marlborough House
Pandora	Two repetitions.
Hebe	Two repetitions, one of which (tinted) is at the R A
Bacchus	R A
Dancing Nymph .	Glasgow
Psyche carrying a cake to Cerebus.	
Wounded Warrior tended by a Woman	Royal Academy
Theseus and the Robber . .	The large model is at the R A The small one, once in Miss Hosmer's possession, is now at Hafod-un-nos

Bassi-Rilievi.

Alexander ordering Homer's Iliad to be placed in the chest taken from Darius	A somewhat high relief in lead; small in size Now at the Royal Institution, Liverpool
Psyche carried by two Zephyrs.	Exhibited at the R A.
Chimney-piece	Designed for Sir John Gladstone
The Meeting of Hero and Leander	Chatsworth Exhibited R A, 1841.
The Hours leading the Horses of the Sun.	Wentworth House His first study in the anatomy of the horse Exhibited R A, 1849
Phaeton driving the Chariot of the Sun.	
Eteocles and Polynices . .	The cast is at the R A It was never executed in marble
Marriage of Psyche and Celestial Love.	Windsor. There are two repetitions
Cupid pursuing Psyche .	Two repetitions Hafod-un-nos.
Eros and Aphrodite .	
Juno conducting Hypnos to Jupiter	Windsor.
Amalthea nursing the child Jupiter.	Castle Howard.
Wounded Amazon on the ground struggling with Horse	Eastham
Cupid and Psyche	R.A. One repetition.

Subject.	Notes and Present Location
Venus and Cupid	Exhibited R.A., 1839 One repetition. Hadzor
Eros and Anteros struggling for the soul.	
Minerva bringing Pegasus to Bellerophon	
Birth of Venus—received by Celestial Love and Crowned by Persuasion.	Not executed in marble. R.A.
Cupid wounding Sappho .	Do
Love between Beauty and Fortune.	Do
Hippolytus	Do.
Venus and Cupid appearing to Sappho to console her	Do.
Love and Idleness	Do
Psyche receiving Nectar from Hebe in the presence of Celestial Love.	Wentworth Hall
Oenone deserted by Paris	Do.
Minerva the Genius of Arts and Manufactures	Design for a gold medal executed by Wyon for a Mr Thomson of Manchester
Christ blessing little Children	His last completed work Hafod-un-nos

Memorials (Bassi-rilievi)

The distribution of Alms (1809)	This is attributed to his employer, Francis, as may be others in the neighbourhood of Liverpool. At Sefton Church
Justice protecting Innocence	In memory of Thomas Earle Liverpool Cemetery Chapel
William Earl, seated, reading the Bible	Liverpool Cemetery Chapel
Blundell Holinshed and his Guardian Angel	Ditto.
Hope (1840)	In memory of Mr and Mrs Edward Roscoe, Ullet Road Church, Liverpool.
An Act of Charity . . .	Liverpool Cemetery Chapel.
A Portrait, seated, of Mrs. Emily Robinson.	Ditto
Angel consoling a Widow and her Children	In memory of Mr Eyre Coote
A Portrait of Mrs H R Sandbach	Hafod-un-nos

Subject	Notes and Present Location
Husband mourning for his Wife with Child in his arms	In memory of Mrs Byrom, at Danesbury, Cheshire.
Angel carrying Child and leading Mother to Heaven	In memory of the Countess of Leicester
Angel receiving the Spirit	In memory of Lady Knightly
Angel leading the Spirit to Heaven	In memory of Mrs Pigott
Angel descending to the Dying	In memory of Mrs Cheney.
Portrait of Richard Wyatt, sculptor.	Rome English Cemetery.
Portrait of Mr Westcar . .	
Portrait of Mrs Huskisson, kneeling	Chichester Cathedral
Angel plucking flowers .	In memory of the Bonomi children, four of whom died in the same week.

Portrait Statues

The Rt. Hon William Huskisson	The first is in the small Greek temple to his memory in the Liverpool Cemetery A repetition at the Royal Exchange, London, and another with some alterations in bronze in front of the Custom House, Liverpool Exhibited R A, 1844.
The Rt Hon. Sir Robert Peel	Westminster Abbey
George Stephenson	Exhibited R A, 1851 St George's Hall, Liverpool
Her Majesty Queen Victoria	Buckingham Palace, and a replica at Osborne They belong to the same period as the group at the Princes Hall, Westminster.
The Rt Rev Van Vildert, Bishop of Durham.	Durham Cathedral
Kirkman Finlay, M.P. . .	Glasgow
Dudley North, M P . . .	
Countess Beauchamp . .	This was executed for the Baroness Bray, Lady Beauchamp's mother, and tinted on the model of his Venus

Portrait Busts.

Subject	Notes and Present Location.
Head of Bacchus .	A copy of a workshop model (1805)
The young Augustus	A copy of the Vatican bust, though comparison may shew it to be a study of the head of John Kemble Walker Art Gallery, Liverpool.
John Kemble . . .	This was made in 1816. There are several replicas
Bust of a young lady (? Mrs Robinson).	Exhibited R A , 1816
Mr Henry Park, Liverpool	Exhibited R A., 1816
Mr. S Watson Taylor, M.P. .	Exhibited R A , 1817
Mr J W W Taylor	Ditto
Mrs. Watson Taylor .	Exhibited R A , 1819
Mr C Ellison, M P .	Exhibited R A , 1822.
A nobleman . . .	Exhibited R A., 1823.
Mr William Roscoe .	Now at the Royal Institution, Liverpool A replica is at the Ullet Road Church, Liverpool
Mr H R Sandbach . .	Hafod-un-nos
Mrs H R Sandbach	Ditto
The Rt Hon Wm Huskisson	
Mrs Mainwaring . .	
Mrs Jameson	
Sir Charles Lyell	
Dhuleep Singh . .	
Grazia filia Capuensis . .	Now at Windsor
Luisa mulier e Sabinis .	
Victoria of Albano	
Sir Charles Eastlake, P R.A	
Duchess of Wellington . .	
Her Majesty Queen Victoria	Exhibited R A , 1848 (one replica)
Viscountess Clifden	
H.M Queen Alexandra . .	Exhibited R A , 1864 Marlborough House.
The Rt Hon Ed Cardwell, M.P	
Mr John Lloyd Wynne	Corwen

Portrait-Bassi-Rilievi.

Subject	Notes and Present Location
Mr William Roscoe . .	Probably his first attempt at portraiture This was extensively copied in plaster A medallion was also cast in bronze.
Mrs. H. R Sandbach on horseback	
Mr W R Sandbach . . .	Now at Hafod-un-nos
Mrs W R. Sandbach . .	Ditto
Mr. John Lloyd Wynne	Rhaggat, Corwen

Bibliography.

Imitations of Drawings by John Gibson, R.A Sculptor. Engraved by G Wenzel and L Prosseda, Rome Oblong Folio.	Hogarth, London 1851
The Story of Psyche With a classical enquiry into the signification of the fable by Elizabeth Strutt, and designs in outline by John Gibson, R A , Sculptor. Folio London	First Edition, 1852 Second Edition, 1857.
Engravings from the Original Compositions of John Gibson, R.A., Sculptor. Rome Drawn by P. Guglielmo Folio	London, 1861
The proportions of the human figure Also a canon of the proportions of the human figure founded upon a diagram invented by John Gibson . With description, practical application, and illustrative outlines by J Bonomi.	London, 1857 There were five editions, the last was issued in 1880 This book is founded upon Lib III. Cap i. of the 'De Architectura' of Vitruvius Pollio. Bonomi published the Latin text with an English translation in 1856, under the title "The Proportions of the Human Figure."

APPENDIX II

GIBSON'S BIRTHPLACE

In view of the controversy as to the place where Gibson was born, it is desirable that the claims of the several places be discussed. This controversy commenced in September 1866—some nine months after his death—when the memorial to the sculptor at Conway Church was mooted. It was lately re-opened[1] subsequent to the valuable educative suggestion made by Mr. A. T. Davies, the Secretary of the Welsh Department of the Board of Education—to name the new school at Gyffin the "John Gibson Memorial School," and that mural decorations be specially designed for the school, in consonance with the ideals of the great artist. This controversy is still proceeding (29th April 1911). The earlier controversy had two results. Lord Lytton, who wrote the inscription on the memorial, changed "born at Conway" to "born near Conway"—which certainly made the epitaph correct. The other result was that a tablet was placed on the Chapel House, attached to the Baptist Chapel at Ffordd Lâs, Llansantffraid Glan

[1] More especially in the *Liverpool Daily Post* and the Welsh weekly *Y Goleuad*

Conwy, Denbighshire, stating that Gibson was born there This was entirely due to the influence of a well-known and able Welsh litterateur, I. D. Ffraid, who summed up the evidence given during the controversy and declared in favour of Ffordd Lâs (*Yr Herald Cymraeg*, 15th Dec. 1866). But it is very doubtful indeed if I. D. Ffraid's decision was the correct one even on the evidence at his disposal.

On the one hand we have the oft-repeated statements of both John and Solomon Gibson as far back as 1839 declaring that John was born at Gyffin—but they do not indicate whether they meant the village or parish of Gyffin. Supporting this we have the following entry in the Conway Parish Register :—

"1790. Baptiz'd John, son of William Gibson of the parish of Gyffin by Jane Roberts his Wife, June 19th."

This entry also corroborates the statement that John Gibson was born at the Gatehouse Benarth, or one of the Benarth Lodges, now pulled down.

On the other hand, seventy-six years after his birth, some eight people declared that he was born at Ffordd Lâs. It is therefore necessary to examine their evidence. It is doubtful whether their evidence is at all satisfactory It seems to be based entirely on the fact that the Gibsons did live at the Chapel House, and that one or two of the sons were born there, but not John. They could only have lived there very few years, for they

returned to the parish of Gyffin and then left for
Liverpool—with the intention of emigrating. This
I think can be made clear later. The confusion is
natural after a long period of time, especially as the
Gibsons lived but for a very little time at Ffordd
Lâs—which is on the opposite side of the estuary
of the Conwy to Gyffin. But the only definite
evidence is in direct conflict with documentary
evidence. One stated that " he and Gibson (both of
them, born in the nineties of that century) used to
play marbles together. It was not until later that
the Gibson family went to Gyffin to live." Now
this is not supported by the Conway Register and
is still further contradicted by the dates, which are
given in the reference to his father's connection
with the Baptist denomination (*Thomas* " History of
the Baptists " (in Welsh),—the Pontypridd edition.)[1]
The year following John's birth, namely 1791,
William Gibson seceded to the Baptists and was
baptized at Ffordd Lâs, by the minister, a certain
John Evans. When John Evans removed to
Dolau in 1792, the Gibsons went to live at the
Chapel House at Ffordd Lâs—and William
Gibson became a local preacher with that body.
Later, in 1795, owing to some friction, they
left Ffordd Lâs and returned to Gyffin. This
account, therefore, of William Gibson's career as a
Baptist preacher in itself destroys the whole of
the evidence in favour of Ffordd Lâs. There
remains the question, as to whether he was born

---

[1] Pp 590—1 Cf also *Spinther James*, Hanes y Bedyddwyr
Vol iii, pp 422-4 The Rev Spinther James had access to certain
documentary evidence confirming this evidence.

at the Gate House, one of the ruined cottages, or Gyffin village. This can, I think, be satisfactorily decided. Mr. Daniel Evans of Wiga, Llangystenin, has certain early letters which indicate that, after their marriage, William Gibson and Jane Roberts (the custom, in Wales, was till lately, for the wife to retain her maiden surname) went to live in a cottage, now ruined, near the home farm of Benarth. It was also near to his wife's home, Fachleidiog. His evidence is confirmed by Mr. Clarence Whaite, P.R.C.A., R.W.S., who was told by a neighbour, whose sister, one Nancy Davies, nursed John Gibson as a child, that he was born in the cottage indicated. The narcissi which bloom in plenty on the spot are still called " William Gibson's flowers "—" blodau William Gibson "—by the neighbouring cottagers Gibson's statement of his only peculation as a child is also proof that as a child he lived outside the walls of Conway. This would account for his continual reference to himself as " John of Conway," while the ruined cottage near Benarth is near enough to that town to justify his statement that he was born near Conway. Again two years before his death he told Mr. T. H. Thomas, R C.A. (Arlunydd Penygarn), of Cardiff, that he was born in the parish of Gyffin, near Conway. There can, therefore, be no hesitation in rejecting the whole of the evidence in favour of Ffordd Lâs noi in accepting the family evidence that he was born in Gyffin—that is in that parish, and *not* on the other side of the estuary of the Conway, in Denbighshire.

INDEX

253

Lightning Source UK Ltd.
Milton Keynes UK
UKOW041127030312

188301UK00001B/65/P